WALKING
LONDON

WALKING
LONDON
THE BEST OF THE CITY

Sara Calian

NATIONAL GEOGRAPHIC

WALKING
LONDON

CONTENTS

PART 1
PAGE 12
WHIRLWIND TOURS

PART 2
PAGE 36
LONDON'S NEIGHBORHOODS

PART 3
PAGE 174
TRAVEL ESSENTIALS

**Previous pages:
Tower Bridge;
left: The Lord
Mayor's Show;
above right: Chelsea
Pensioners at the
Royal Hospital
Chelsea; right:
Statue of Eros in
Piccadilly Circus**

Introduction

Samuel Johnson, the great British writer, once said that he who tires of London tires of life. I've never tired of the city, though it has frequently left me exhausted. Because—mostly—I walk it. I've done so since I was unleashed on its streets at age 14 in the '60s. It was the Beatles' London then. Jazzed. Experimental. Full of life. Pretty much as it is today, but with a different cultural idiom, revolutionary architecture, and draconian traffic restrictions. The one thing that endures: The best way to experience this great city is to hoof it.

Navigate a city on foot and you feel, intimately, its energy. You connect with the place. You engage face to face with its inhabitants. Neighborhoods become neighborly, and storefronts draw you close. You begin to sense its cadence—where its energy ebbs and flows. You smell the flowers, read the fine print on monuments, stumble across local celebrations, lounge on park lawns, eavesdrop on workaday conversations, succumb to a nightclub beat, randomly sample an early morning espresso, or simply sit and watch as life passes by in natural high-def. While cars and cyclists must hew to a mostly prescribed route, walkers can ramble, divert, explore, linger, and follow their noses. Happenstance is the currency of the traveler who chooses to go step by step.

The Millennium Bridge links Tate Modern and the Globe theater on the south bank of the Thames to the City on the north side.

This book celebrates the art of the city walk. We invite you step out and navigate—we'll be with you stride for stride.

Keith Bellows

Editor-in-Chief, National Geographic Traveler *magazine*

Visiting London

London is one of the world's most culturally rich and dynamic cities, but with 7.5 million residents and 27 million visitors per year and an area of 607 square miles (1,600 sq km), it can be one of the most bewildering, even for seasoned travelers.

London in a Nutshell

From the time of the first Roman city (founded in A.D. 50) to today's modern metropolis, the River Thames has been at the heart of London. For centuries, it was the main highway for Londoners, and a boat trip or a walk along its pedestrianized South Bank still provides a great to way to understand the city. The Tower of London, St. Paul's Cathedral, Westminster's Houses of Parliament, and Tate Britain are all on the north bank, while a string of cultural institutions (the Globe Theatre, Tate Modern, and the South Bank arts complex) line the revitalized south side.

Navigating London

London's layout can be confusing—some streets twist and turn to a bewildering degree, and many look similar to each other—but there

London Day-by-Day

Monday Most sites are open except for Sir John Soane's Museum, Whitechapel Gallery, and Apsley House. Entrance to the Courtauld Gallery is free until 2 p.m.

Tuesday Most sites are open except for Apsley House. The British Library is open until 9 p.m.

Wednesday All sites open.

Thursday All sites open. The British Museum is open until 8:30 p.m.

Friday Most public galleries are open late, including the National Gallery (until 9 p.m.), the Victoria and Albert Museum (until 10 p.m.), and Tate Modern (until 10 p.m.). Spitalfields and Borough markets are open.

Saturday Museums and galleries are open, but the Old Bailey and the Houses of Parliament are closed. Tate Modern is open until 10 p.m. Portobello, Camden Lock, and Borough markets are all open.

Sunday Most museums and galleries are open, but Sir John Soane's Museum, the Old Bailey, and the Houses of Parliament are closed. Westminster Abbey and St. Paul's are open to worshipers but closed to sightseers. Most theaters are closed except the Globe. Shops are open between noon and 6 p.m. Spitalfields, Petticoat Lane, and Brick Lane markets are open.

Two of London's most famous icons are outlined against a rare blue sky—the city's reputation for changeable weather is justified, so do pack an umbrella and raincoat.

are some tricks to navigating this enormous city on foot.

Many Londoners carry a pocket-size *London A-Z* street guide whenever they leave home. If you get lost and you don't have a map, find a bus stop. All bus stops have a map of the local area. See which bus stop you're at (look for the red circle with white lettering at the top of the pole), find your bus stop on the map, and you'll know your location.

Don't rely on the river for orientation. Although most of central London is on the north side of the Thames, the river twists and turns so much that it is not reliable for direction.

If you are looking across the Thames at Westminster, for example, you are in fact looking east, not south.

Crossing the Road

Jaywalking is not an offense in the U.K., and pedestrians are free to use their own judgment when crossing the street—but this is not a license to step out into traffic. Vehicles drive on the left side of the road, so you need to look to your right first before crossing—except when you are on a one-way street. And watch out particularly for cyclists because they hug the curbside, travel silently, and often ignore traffic signals.

Using This Guide

Each tour—which might be only a walk, or might take advantage of the city's
public transportation as well—is plotted on a map and has been planned to take
into account opening hours and the times of day when sites are less crowded.
Many end near restaurants, theaters, or lively night spots for evening activities.

Whirlwind Tours

Whirlwind Tours are for people who have only a day or a weekend to spend in the city and want to be sure that they see the best of the best. Choose your tour based on your time and interests: One Day; Weekend (Day 1 & Day 2); For Fun; and With Kids (Day 1 & Day 2).

Tips For the Day and Weekend Tours, a Tips spread following the itinerary map provides insider information on detours from the key sites, extra places to see, nearby cafés and restaurants, and ideas for adapting the tours to suit your interests.

Site Descriptions For the For Fun and With Kids Tours, key sites spreads following the maps provide descriptions of all the sites and practical information for visitors.

Neighborhood Tours

The nine neighborhood tours each begin with an introduction, followed by an itinerary map highlighting the key sites that make up the tour and detailed key sites descriptions. Each tour is followed by an "in-depth" spread showcasing one major site along the route, a "distinctly" London spread providing background information on a quintessential element of that neighborhood, and a "best of" spread that groups sites thematically.

Itinerary Map A map of the neighborhood shows the locations of the key sites, Tube stations, and main streets.

Captions These briefly describe the key sites and give instructions on finding the next site on the tour. Page references direct you to full descriptions of the key sites on the following pages.

Route Dotted lines link the key sites.

Price Ranges for Key Sites

£	under £3
££	£4–£7
£££	£7–£11
££££	£12–£15
£££££	over £15

Prices Ranges for Good Eats (for one person, excluding drinks)

£	under £12
££	£12–£20
£££	£20–£30
££££	£30–£50
£££££	over £50

Good Eats Refer to these lists for a selection of cafés and restaurants along the tour.

Key Sites Descriptions Following the order of the tour, these provide a detailed description and highlights for each site, plus address, website, phone number, entrance fee, days closed, and nearest Tube station.

PART 1

Whirlwind Tours

London in a Day

Get an overview of London's sights with this packed one-day tour.

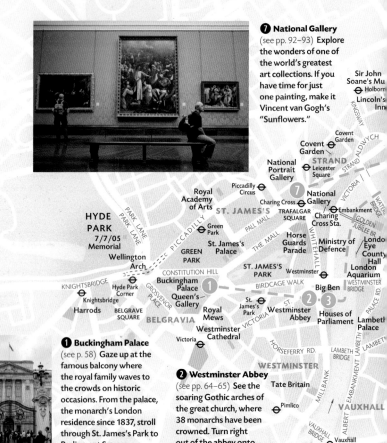

⑦ National Gallery
(see pp. 92–93) **Explore
the wonders of one of
the world's greatest
art collections. If you
have time for just
one painting, make it
Vincent van Gogh's
"Sunflowers."**

❶ Buckingham Palace
(see p. 58) **Gaze up at the
famous balcony where
the royal family waves to
the crowds on historic
occasions. From the palace,
the monarch's London
residence since 1837, stroll
through St. James's Park to
Parliament Square.**

❷ Westminster Abbey
(see pp. 64–65) **See the
soaring Gothic arches of
the great church, where
38 monarchs have been
crowned. Turn right
out of the abbey onto
Parliament Square.**

**LONDON IN A DAY   DISTANCE: 6.5 MILES (10.4 KM)
TIME: APPROX. 8 HOURS   TUBE START: HYDE PARK CORNER**

6 St. Paul's Cathedral
(see pp. 48–49) Climb 528 steps,
past the Whispering Gallery, for
a panoramic view of London.
Catch a No. 15 heritage bus west
toward Trafalgar Square.

5 Tower Bridge (see
pp. 162–163) Visit the
Victorian engine rooms
to admire the gleaming
machinery. Cross to the
south bank of the river and
follow the Thames Path
west to the Millennium
Bridge, then cross north for
St. Paul's Cathedral.

4 Tower of London (see
pp. 168–169) Yeoman Warders
and the Crown Jewels are
just some of the sights in this
well-preserved royal fortress,
founded by King William the
Conqueror in 1066. Walk up
the steps leading to Tower
Bridge Approach.

3 Houses of Parliament
(see pp. 58–59) Big
Ben's clock tower is an
unmistakable landmark
at the northern end of
this Victorian Gothic
masterpiece. Step down to
Westminster Pier for the
river taxi going east.

Tips

These are the best of the best London sights. All are described elsewhere in the book—just follow the cross-references for more detailed information. The tips here provide advice on visiting these major sights when you have limited time. They also include additional sights nearby and places to eat.

❶ Buckingham Palace (see p. 58) If you want to know more about the bearskin-hat-wearing guards, head to the ■ GUARDS MUSEUM (*Wellington Barracks, Birdcage Walk, SW1, www.the guardsmuseum.com, 020 7414 3271, ££, closed public holidays and for other events*), which has artifacts from the five regiments that guard the palace.

City Hall, home to the London Assembly, was designed by architect Norman Foster.

❷ Westminster Abbey (see pp. 64–65) After exploring the abbey, visit ■ THE VICTORIA TOWER GARDENS (*Abingdon St., SW1*), adjacent to the Houses of Parliament. It's a peaceful park by the river that includes the ■ BUXTON MEMORIAL FOUNTAIN, which celebrates the emancipation of slaves in the British Empire in 1834.

❸ Houses of Parliament (see pp. 58–59) The Houses of Parliament's bells ring every 15 minutes, but ■ BIG BEN only chimes on the hour—stick around to hear its sonorous toll. A quick alternative to a tour around Parliament is the 700-year-old ■ JEWEL TOWER (*Abingdon St., SW1, www.english-heritage.org.uk, 0870 333 1181, £, closed Jan.1, Dec. 24–26*), which used to store royal jewels and now has displays on the history of Parliament. The fastest way to travel on the river is to use the ■ THAMES

CLIPPERS river taxis (see p. 30). For a more leisurely option, take one of the tour boats where guides bring the river to life with interesting facts and lively tales from the river's past.

❹ Tower of London (see pp. 168–169) Expect hour-long lines to get into the Tower of London. If you don't have time to wait, visit ■ ALL HALLOWS BY THE TOWER (*Byward St., EC3, www.ahbtt .org.uk, 020 7481 2928*), a Saxon abbey built in A.D. 675. Sixth U.S. president John Quincy Adams was married here in 1797. Check out a nearby original section of the ■ LONDON WALL just outside Tower Hill tube station. Dating from around A.D. 225, the 35-foot-high (10.7 m) wall defined the city's boundaries for more than a thousand years. If your feet are feeling tired, ■ TRINITY SQUARE, just north of the Tower, is a good place for a rest. The square was the site of most of London's public executions. It has a memorial to sailors lost during the two World Wars.

❺ Tower Bridge (see pp. 162–163) ■ ST. KATHARINE DOCKS, just east of Tower Bridge, has excellent cafés and restaurants, making it a great place for lunch. In summer, you can enjoy free films, plays, and musical performances at ■ THE SCOOP, the London Assembly building's 800-seat

CUSTOMIZING **YOUR DAY**

If you want to squeeze some shopping into your day, the One New Change shopping center *(One New Change, EC4, www.onenewchange.com)*, to the east of St. Paul's Cathedral, has fashion stores and jewelry and gift shops. Or you could get off the No. 15 bus on the Strand and walk through to the shops in Covent Garden (see p. 102).

outdoor amphitheater on the bridge's south side.

❻ St. Paul's Cathedral (see pp. 48–49) After touring the cathedral, head to nearby ■ ST. BARTHOLOMEW'S HOSPITAL (*West Smithfield, EC1, www. bartsandthelondon.nhs.uk, 020 7377 7000*). Founded in 1123, it's Britain's oldest hospital, though most of the current building dates from the 18th century. Look for the plaque commemorating the death of Scottish hero William Wallace (aka Braveheart), who was executed near here in 1305.

❼ National Gallery (see pp. 92–93) After gazing at paintings by artists such as Paul Cézanne, Claude Monet, and Vincent van Gogh, dine in the gallery's ■ NATIONAL CAFÉ (see p. 140), which remains open even after the gallery has closed.

WHIRLWIND TOURS

London in a Weekend

Spend your first day touring museums and palaces, and enjoying exquisite shopping and wonderful views.

❶ Madame Tussauds (see p. 22)
For nearly 200 years, wax models have enthralled, shocked, and at times appalled visitors. Take the Tube to Knightsbridge.

❷ Harrods (see pp. 146–147)
London's most famous store has a food court sumptuous enough to satisfy any palate. Walk west on Brompton Road.

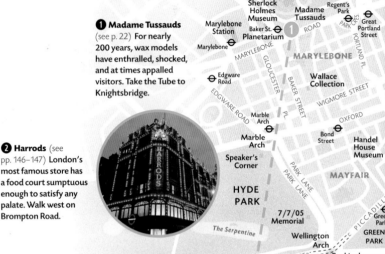

REGENT'S PARK

Sherlock Holmes Museum
Madame Tussauds
Regent's Park
Great Portland Street

Marylebone Station
Baker St. ❶
Planetarium
ROAD

Marylebone
MARYLEBONE

MARYLEBONE

GLOUCESTER PL.
BAKER STREET
PORTLAND PL.

Edgware Road

Wallace Collection

WIGMORE STREET

EDGWARE ROAD

Marble Arch

OXFORD

Marble Arch

Bond Street

Handel House Museum

Speaker's Corner

PARK LANE
PARK LANE

MAYFAIR

HYDE PARK

7/7/05 Memorial

PICCADILLY

The Serpentine

Wellington Arch

Green Park

GREEN PARK

KENSINGTON GORE
KENSINGTON RD.
KNIGHTSBRIDGE
Hyde Park Corner
Buckingham Palace ❹

Royal Albert Hall

Royal College of Music
Science Museum

EXHIBITION RD.
Victoria & Albert Museum

KNIGHTSBRIDGE
Knightsbridge
❷ Harrods

Queen's Gallery
Royal Mews

BELGRAVE SQUARE

Natural History Museum ❸
Hampton & Kew
CROMWELL ROAD

THURLOE PL.
BROMPTON ROAD

BROMPTON

SLOANE STREET

BELGRAVIA

EATON SQ.
Victoria
Victoria Station

Gloucester Road
South Kensington

Sloane Square

Victoria Coach Station

❸ Natural History Museum (see pp. 136–137)
Be awed by the size of a blue whale, scared by the teeth of a *T. rex*, or fascinated by a stuffed polar bear. Take the Tube to St. James's Park.

❹ Buckingham Palace (see p. 58)
As well as admiring the palace, check out the marble memorial to Queen Victoria out front. Walk through St. James's Park, then south on Storey's Gate.

LONDON IN A WEEKEND, DAY 1 DISTANCE: 6 MILES (9.5 KM)
TIME: APPROX. 7.5 HOURS TUBE START: BAKER STREET

WHIRLWIND TOURS

8 Trafalgar Square
(see p. 88) London's favorite public space, used for rallies and celebrations, is also full of public art such as a 170-foot-high (52 m) memorial to Admiral Lord Nelson, who defeated the combined French and Spanish fleets at Trafalgar in 1805.

7 London Eye (see p. 74) Admire the view from London's 40-story-high (135 m) observation wheel. Cross the Golden Jubilee Footbridge, which flanks Hungerford Bridge, and walk west on Northumberland Avenue.

6 Houses of Parliament (see pp. 58–59) Big Ben, cast in 1858 at the Whitechapel Bell Foundry (which also cast the Liberty Bell in Philadelphia), chimes on the hour every hour. Cross Westminster Bridge and take the steps to the London Eye.

5 Westminster Abbey (see pp. 64–65) Visit the royal family's most important church, where Prince William and Kate Middleton were married. Cross over Abingdon Street.

2

DAY

London in a Weekend

*Spend your second day visiting a
medieval castle, a baroque cathedral, a graceful bridge,
and a Victorian market.*

❶ Shakespeare's Globe (see p. 76) **Start the day with a
tour of the reconstructed Globe Theatre, built on the site
where William Shakespeare's plays were performed more
than 400 years ago. Head north across the Millennium
Bridge to St. Paul's Cathedral.**

❻ Tate Modern (see
pp. 78–79) **End the day
with a quick look around
the Turbine Hall—one of
London's largest gallery
spaces, which hosts
specially commissioned
exhibitions from
contemporary artists.**

Chancery
Gray's Lane
Inn
HIGH HOLBORN
Lincoln's
Inn

Royal Courts
of Justice
ALDWYCH FLEET
Temple
Somerset EMBANKMENT
House
Thames
VICTORIA WATERLOO BRIDGE National
Theatre
GOLDEN
JUBILEE BR. Royal
Festival Hall
London Waterloo
Eye County
Hall Waterloo
London Station
Aquarium
WESTMINSTER BR. WESTMINSTER Lambeth
North
LAMBETH PALACE RD.
Lambeth
Palace ROAD
LAMBETH
LAMBETH

**LONDON IN A WEEKEND, DAY 2   DISTANCE: 3.5 MILES (5.5 KM)
TIME: APPROX. 8 HOURS   TUBE START: MANSION HOUSE**

2 St. Paul's Cathedral (see pp. 48–49) Attend a morning service at London's largest church. Take the Tube two stops east to Liverpool Street.

3 Old Spitalfields Market Enjoy lunch at one of this Victorian market's many eateries, before browsing the shops and stalls for the perfect gift or souvenir. Walk south on Commercial Street and then Mansell Street.

4 Tower of London (see pp. 168–169) London's 11th-century castle has something for everyone—historic armor, the Crown Jewels, and grisly stories from the tower's past. Walk up the steps to Tower Bridge Approach.

5 Tower Bridge (see pp. 162–163) A combination of Victorian engineering excellence and architectural splendor makes this one of the world's most memorable bridges. Cross to the river's south bank, and walk west along the Thames Path.

Tips

These major London sights can be seen in two days. Refer to the cross-references for detailed information elsewhere in the book. There's also information here on detours to nearby sights, on local cafés and restaurants, and suggestions for customizing the tour to suit your own interests.

WHIRLWIND TOURS

DAY 1

❶ Madame Tussauds If it's a sunny day, walk south on Baker Street and west on Oxford Street to Marble Arch and continue south through ■ HYDE PARK (see p. 138), one of London's largest green spaces and a former royal hunting ground, to Harrods.

Londoners relax and picnic in Hyde Park.

❷ Harrods (see pp. 146–147) Eat ■ BRUNCH here, either in one of the store's many restaurants or in the wonderfully varied food hall.

❸ Natural History Museum (see pp. 136–137) If the Natural History Museum doesn't pique your interest, the ■ SCIENCE MUSEUM (see pp. 132–133) or the ■ VICTORIA AND ALBERT MUSEUM (see pp. 130–131) are excellent alternatives.

❼ London Eye (see p. 74) After riding on the Eye, bibliophiles can make a detour along the river past the Royal Festival Hall (see p. 74) to the ■ SOUTH BANK BOOK MARKET, an open-air market selling a large range of secondhand books (open until around 7 p.m.). A little farther east is the arty enclave of ■ GABRIEL'S WHARF (*56 Upper Ground, SE1, www.coinstreet.org*), with craft shops, galleries, cafés, and great views of the river.

❽ Trafalgar Square (see p. 88) Admire some of the sculpture on Trafalgar Square, including a statue of first U.S. president ■ **GEORGE WASHINGTON**, whose plinth in front of the National Gallery stands on earth imported from Virginia in honor of Washington's pledge to never set foot on British soil. Finish your day with dinner in the crypt of ■ **ST. MARTIN-IN-THE-FIELDS** (see p. 89) before attending a concert of baroque music in the church. Many of the concerts are held by candlelight.

DAY 2

❸ Old Spitalfields Market (*105a Commercial St., E1, www .visitspitalfields.com, 020 7375 2963, closed Mon.–Wed. and Sat.*) If you can't find what you're looking for at Spitalfields market, try nearby ■ **BRICK LANE** (see pp. 163–164), whose Sunday market is popular for chic clothing and bric-a-brac.

❹ Tower of London (see pp. 168–169) You can walk around three sides of the Tower of London, getting a great view of the walls without having to go in. On the river side, you can see ■ **TRAITOR'S GATE**, ■ **TOWER BRIDGE**, and a display of historic cannon.

CUSTOMIZING **YOUR DAY**

With at least one night in London, why not check out some of Europe's best evening entertainments? Enjoy a performance at the Royal Opera House in Covent Garden (see pp. 102–103) or modern drama at the National Theatre (see p. 75), or visit a small rock club in Soho. To find out what's going on, pick up a copy of *Time Out*, the weekly listings magazine.

---

❺ Tower Bridge (see pp. 162–163) ■ **BUTLER'S WHARF** (see p. 77) on the south side of the bridge has good restaurants and is a fine place to stop for lunch. On the walk along the river, you can make a detour south to the ■ **OLD OPERATING THEATRE** (*9a St. Thomas St., SE1, www.the garret.org.uk, ££, closed Dec. 15–Jan. 5*), a short way south of London Bridge. This purpose-built theater in a garret over a hospital's church dates back to 1822 and has displays covering the history of surgery and nursing.

❻ Tate Modern (see pp. 78–79) Even if you are not interested in contemporary art, pop in to see the ■ **TURBINE HALL**, a massive open space running the length of the building and extending up to the roof. The bridge across the hall at first-floor level is a good viewpoint.

London for Fun

*After a busy day of outings and shopping, relax with
an English afternoon tea before an evening at the theater.*

❷ Grays Antiques
(see p. 26) Pick up a
souvenir from this
eclectic selection
of vintage objects.
Head south on Davies
Street, then east on
Brook Street and
Hanover Street to
Regent Street.

**❸ Regent Street
Shopping** (see p. 26)
More retail-therapy awaits
behind the facades of
architect John Nash's 19th-
century thoroughfare. At
the foot of Regent Street,
walk south on Swallow
Street and then west on
Piccadilly.

❶ Knightsbridge Shopping (see
pp. 26, 146–147, 156–157) **Shopping**
at Harrods and snacking at its
famous food hall are a must before
tackling the designer stores nearby.
Take the Tube to Bond Street.

**LONDON FOR FUN DISTANCE: 6.8 MILES (11 KM)
TIME: APPROX. 8.5 HOURS TUBE START: SOUTHWARK**

❻ American Bar at the Savoy (see p. 27) Quaff well-earned drinks at one of London's best bars. The Savoy Theatre is next door.

❼ Savoy Theatre (see p. 27) Catch a musical in this delightfully decorated art deco building.

❺ No. 15 Heritage Bus (see p. 27) Enjoy a ride on a classic 1960s Routemaster double-decker bus. Get off at The Savoy.

❹ Fortnum & Mason (see pp. 27, 69) Sipping afternoon tea while nibbling on clotted cream scones and listening to an excellent pianist is a quintessential British experience. Walk east to Regent Street and turn south to Pall Mall, then east to Trafalgar Square.

Gray's Inn
Farringdon Station
Chancery Lane
Farringdon
HOLBORN
Smithfield Market
HOLBORN VIA.
Lincoln's Inn
Royal Courts of Justice
City Thameslink
Dr. Johnson's House
FLEET STREET
Temple
Temple
Blackfriars Sta.
Blackfriars
VICTORIA EMBANKMENT
BLACKFRIARS BRIDGE
Thames
NORTH
National Theatre
SOUTHWARK
STAMFORD ST.
Royal Festival Hall
Southwark
Waterloo
Waterloo Station
Lambeth North

Harrods' food hall has counters dedicated to tea, cheese, meat, bread, chocolate, and more.

Knightsbridge Shopping

1 Knightsbridge's streets hold London's hottest designer shops, including **Dior** (*31 Sloane St.*), **Louis Vuitton** (*190–192 Sloane St.*), **Chanel** (*167–170 Sloane St.*), **Giorgio Armani** (*37–42 Sloane St.,*), and **Prada** (*43–45 Sloane St.*). You can pick up some great shoes, too, at **Jimmy Choo** (*32 Sloane St.,*). There are also some opulent department stores, such as **Harrods** (see p. 146–147), which has a fabulous food hall as well as 60 high-end fashion departments.

Knightsbridge, SW1 • Tube: Knightsbridge

Grays Antiques

2 Tucked between Oxford Street and Bond Street, Grays's 200 dealers offer a wide selection of antiques, such as Oriental ceramics, coins, vintage fashion, and teddy bears. A number of dealers, including **The Gilded Lily, Jo Elton & Olly Gerrish,** and **Linda Bee,** specialize in jewelry.

58 Davies St. and 1–7 Davies Mews, W1 • www.graysantiques.com • 020 7629 7034 • Closed Sun. • Tube: Bond Street

Regent Street Shopping

3 Regent Street's facades date from the 19th century, with one major exception—**Liberty**'s 1920s black-and-white Tudor-style frontage on the corner of Great Marlborough Street. The store is synonymous with eclectic fashion and jewelry design. The street's central section brims with fashion stores, including **Anthropologie** (*No. 158*), **Aquascutum** (*No. 100*), **Austin Reed** (*Nos. 103–113*), **Karen Millen** (*No. 247*), and **Burberry** (*Nos. 121–123*). The **National Geographic** store (*Nos. 83–97*) has a photo gallery and café.

Regent St., W1 • www.regentstreetonline.com • Tube: Piccadilly Circus

WHIRLWIND TOURS

Fortnum & Mason

4 For the most civilized way to rest your feet in London, head for the fourth floor of Fortnum & Mason, where St. James's Restaurant takes afternoon tea very seriously. Sample sumptuous scones served with clotted cream and your choice of preserve, canapés, and a selection of sandwiches. There are also 130 types of tea available. A pianist plays gentle music in the afternoons, while the dress code requests "both sexes lean more towards elegance."

181 Piccadilly, W1 • www.fortnumandmason.com • 020 7734 8040 • ££££ • Closed Jan. 1 and Dec. 25 • Tube: Piccadilly Circus

No. 15 Heritage Bus

5 Jump through the open back of a 1960s-era Routemaster bus, which has been preserved by the city. The No. 15 heritage bus service, whose experienced conductors are happy to answer your questions, runs every 15 minutes between Trafalgar Square and Tower Hill, along a section of the regular No. 15 route.

Trafalgar Sq. • www.tfl.gov.uk • 0845 300 7000 • £ • Last bus at 6:30 p.m.

American Bar at The Savoy

6 Abundant olives and snacks are served with expertly mixed cocktails, while a pianist plays classic American jazz in this vibrantly decorated bar, evocative of the 1920s.

The Strand • www.fairmont.com/savoy • 020 7836 4343 • Tube: Charing Cross

Savoy Theatre

7 Finish the day by catching a musical or a lighthearted comedy at this Victorian auditorium, the first to be lit with electricity, which was rebuilt in 1929 in art deco style.

The Strand • www.savoy-theatre.co.uk • 0870 1648787 • Tube: Charing Cross

IN **THE KNOW**

Savoy Court, leading to the Savoy Theatre, is the subject of a law forcing traffic to drive on the street's right-hand side, as opposed to the normal left, so theatergoers can exit a taxi and walk straight inside.

London in a Weekend with Kids

London has a tremendous amount to offer children, from haunted castles to stimulating art and thrilling theme parks.

❶ London Eye (see pp. 30, 74)
Take a slow whirl on the giant wheel in the sky for a bird's-eye introduction to the United Kingdom's capital. Hop on a river taxi going east and travel to Tower Millennium Pier.

**LONDON WITH KIDS, DAY 1   DISTANCE: 5.2 MILES (8.3 KM)
TIME: APPROX. 8 HOURS   TUBE START: WATERLOO**

2 Tower of London (see pp. 30, 168–169) A thousand years of British history come alive inside this riverside castle, once home to kings and queens and now the alleged haunt of many a royal ghost. Head up the stairs by the river to get to Tower Bridge Approach.

3 Tower Bridge (see pp. 30, 162–163) London's trademark span offers a superb perch from which to photograph the city. After crossing the bridge, turn west along the Queen's Walk.

4 H.M.S. *Belfast* (see pp. 30, 171) Battle-tested in several wars, this cruiser shows what life is like on the high seas. Walk down narrow Battle Bridge Lane and hang a right onto Tooley Street.

7 Millennium Bridge (see p. 31) Finish the day with a great view of the buildings that line the river, including St. Paul's Cathedral on the north side of the river.

6 Tate Modern (see pp. 31, 78–79) Get a crash course in contemporary art inside a massive old power station. Millennium Bridge is just outside.

5 London Dungeon (see p. 30) Prepare to be scared at this ghoulish blend of theme park and wax museum. Continue west on Tooley and Montague Streets, veering right onto Cathedral Street and back to the Thames Path.

London Eye

1 Take the first ride (10 a.m.) and soar 443 feet (135 m) into the morning sky for city views, with the river right at your feet.

Westminster Bridge Rd., SE1 • www.londoneye.com • 0871 781 3000 • £££££ • Closed Dec. 25 • Tube: Waterloo

Tower of London

2 Be dazzled by the Crown Jewels, spooked by tales of ghosts, and regaled with gruesome stories by the red-uniformed Yeoman Warders—and watch out for snack-stealing ravens.

Tower Hill, EC3 • www.hrp.org.uk • 020 3166 6000 • £££££ • Closed Jan. 1 and Dec. 25–26 • Tube: Tower Hill

Tower Bridge

3 Walk across London's most photographed bridge, or watch the occasional raising and lowering of the roadway that allows large vessels to navigate up and down the Thames.

Tower Bridge Rd., SE1 • www.towerbridge.org.uk • 020 7403 3761 • Exhibition: ££ • Exhibition closed Dec. 24–26 • Tube: Tower Hill

SAVVY **TRAVELER**

The river is the best way to get from the London Eye to the Tower of London. Thames Clippers river taxis (*www.thamesclippers.com,* email: *web@thamesclippers .com)* regularly depart from Waterloo Pier next to the Eye.

H.M.S. *Belfast*

4 Explore this World War II cruiser. Audio guides include a children's version.

Thames Path, off Tooley St., SE1 • http://hmsbelfast.iwm .org.uk • 020 7940 6300 • £££ • Closed Dec. 24–26 • Tube: London Bridge

London Dungeon

5 This macabre attraction will scare you to your bones, with rides such as the **Ride To Hell,** which takes you through the Tower of London's Traitor's Gate.

28–34 Tooley St., SE1 • www.the-dungeons.co.uk • 020 7403 7221 • £££££ • Closed Dec. 25 • Tube: London Bridge

A river cruise from the London Eye to the Tower of London and Tower Bridge

Tate Modern

6 Older children will love exploring this sprawling gallery of contemporary art. Take them to see Roy Lichtenstein's **"Whaam!"** on Level 5. Its comic-book portrayal of a fighter jet shooting a missile is often appreciated by kids. Younger ones will enjoy the nearby **Under 5s Zone,** which has a musical slide, a cubist-inspired mirrored house, and interactive visual displays.

25 Sumner St., SE1 • www.tate.org.uk • 020 7887 8888 • Closed Dec. 24–26 • Tube: Southwark

Millennium Bridge

7 Cross London's newest bridge (destroyed by Death Eaters in the opening scenes of *Harry Potter and the Half-Blood Prince*) for views of the river and of St. Paul's Cathedral on the north bank. If your kids still have the energy, climb 259 steps to the cathedral's **Whispering Gallery,** where whispers travel around the dome.

Linking Tate Modern and St. Paul's Cathedral, SE1 • Tube: Southwark

London in a Weekend with Kids

No child visiting London should miss Hamleys toy shop and Pollock's Toy Museum, or the Egyptian mummies at the British Museum.

0 ———— 1 mile
0 ———— 1 kilometer

❶ **St. James's Park** (see pp. 34, 138) Snap photos of nearby Buckingham Palace and commune with the resident pelicans in this former royal hunting preserve. Exit the park's east end and cross Horse Guards Road.

❷ **Horse Guards** (see pp. 34, 60–61) Some of Britain's best pageantry, such as Trooping the Colour and Changing the Guard, are performed on this parade ground. Turn right onto the Mall and duck beneath the imposing Admiralty Arch.

LONDON WITH KIDS, DAY 2   DISTANCE: 3.7 MILES (6 KM)
TIME: APPROX. 8 HOURS   TUBE START: ST JAMES'S PARK

8 British Museum (see pp. 35, 120–123) **Finish off the day by visiting the ancient statues and Egyptian mummies at one of the world's great museums.**

HOLBORN
Gray's Inn — Chancery Lane
HOLBORN
Sir John Soane's Mus. — HOLBORN VIA
Lincoln's Inn
City Thameslink — St. Paul's
Royal
Courts — FLEET STREET — St. Paul's
of Justice — Temple — Cathedral
Temple — Blackfriars
— Blackfriars Sta.
VICTORIA EMBANKMENT
Somerset — Thames
House
WATERLOO BRIDGE
National — NORTH
Theatre — SOUTHWARK
STAMFORD ST.
Royal Festival Hall
Waterloo
County — Waterloo
Hall — Station
London
Aquarium

Lambeth
Palace
LAMBETH ROAD

LAMBETH

7 Pollock's Toy Museum (see pp. 35, 118) **Travel back to bygone fun and games at a petite museum named after the last of the great Victorian toy-theater makers. Walk south on Tottenham Court Road and east on Great Russell Street.**

3 Trafalgar Square (see pp. 34, 88) **One has to wonder what Admiral Lord Nelson would say about the rabble-rousers, revelers, and sunbathers who so often inhabit his square. Follow the busy Strand east to Southampton Street, and walk two blocks north.**

6 Hamleys (see p. 35) **Britain's oldest and largest toy store bursts at the seams with amusements for all ages. Continue on Regent Street to Oxford Circus station, and take the Tube two stops to Goodge Street.**

5 Piccadilly Circus (see pp. 35, 90) **Six busy roads come together beneath the giant neon signs and a winged Eros statue hunting for would-be lovers. Follow the broad sweep of Regent Street north from the circus.**

4 Covent Garden (see pp. 34, 102) **This one-time fruit, flower, and vegetable market now blooms with street performers and excellent eateries. Head west on Long Acre to reach Leicester Square and Piccadilly Circus.**

St. James's Park

1 This 58-acre (23.4 ha) park is one of London's most kid-friendly spaces. Eat breakfast at **Inn The Park,** where pancakes and a full English breakfast are among the options. There's a playground near the western end, but most children are content to ramble across the lawns, watch the aquatic birdlife (ducks, pelicans, and swans), or scamper across the Blue Bridge to **Duck Island.**

The Mall, SW1 • www.royalparks.gov.uk • 020 7930 1793 • Tube: St. James's Park

Horse Guards

2 Household Cavalry dressed in smart uniforms parade on a ground where knights once jousted. Changing the Guard takes place daily at 11 a.m. (10 a.m. on Sunday).

Whitehall, SW1 • Tube: Westminster or Piccadilly Circus

Trafalgar Square

3 Britain's most renowned public space is a venue for live music, dance performances, art festivals, and the annual New Year's Eve celebrations. Visit the **National Gallery** (see pp. 92–93), on the north side, to see George Stubbs' portrait of the prized horse **Whistlejacket.**

Trafalgar Sq., WC2 • www.london.gov.uk/trafalgarsquare • Tube: Charing Cross

Covent Garden

4 Grab a bite to eat as mimes, acrobats, stunt cyclists, and chainsaw maestros entertain you. If you've got time, visit the **London Transport Museum** (see p. 103) in the market's southeastern corner, where your kids can get behind the wheel of an Tube train simulator and see trains and buses from the 19th century.

Covent Garden Piazza, WC2 • www.coventgardenlondonuk.com • 0870 780 5001 • Tube: Covent Garden or Leicester Square

Piccadilly Circus

5 Famous for its neon signs, the square is also home to kids' favorite **Ripley's Believe It or Not!,** which has a selection of unusual objects such as Marilyn Monroe's makeup box (*1 Piccadilly Circus, W1, www.ripleyslondon.com, 020 3238 0022, £££££*).

Piccadilly Circus, W1 • Tube: Piccadilly Circus

Hamleys

6 Founded in 1760, this gargantuan toy shop has just about every toy, from Barbie to Thomas the Tank Engine. They have a particularly incredible selection of Lego, including a scale model of Tower Bridge. The staff enjoys showing off the toys, making it lots of fun to walk around the store.

188–196 Regent St., W1• www.hamleys.com • 0871 704 1977 • Closed Dec. 25 • Tube: Piccadilly Circus

Pollock's Toy Museum

7 Vintage toys from around the world fill this small museum. Highlights include Egyptian clay toys, a 19th-century rocking horse, porcelain dolls, dollhouses, and mechanical toys from the olden days.

1 Scala St., W1 • www.pollockstoymuseum.com • 020 7636 3452 • ££ • Closed Sun. • Tube: Goodge Street

British Museum

8 The museum offers several "family trails" as well as hands-on desks, where kids can handle objects from the collection. Young ones will be fascinated by the **Egyptian mummies,** especially the mumified cat (Room 62–63), and the **Easter Island heads** (Room 24).

38 Russell Sq., WC1 • www.britishmuseum.org • 020 7323 8299 • Closed Jan. 1 and Dec. 24–26 • Tube: Holborn

The British Museum provides free activity packs to entertain children during their visit.

PART 2

London's Neighborhoods

London's Neighborhoods

King's Cross Station
King's Cross
St. Pancras
St. Pancras Station
GRAY'S INN ROAD
KING'S CROSS ROAD
ST. PANCRAS

Bloomsbury **112**

Russell Square
SOUTHAMPTON ROW
BLOOMSBURY
British Museum

CLERKENWELL
ST. JOHN STREET
GOSWELL ROAD
OLD
Old St.
STREET
CITY ROAD

FINSBURY
CLERKENWELL ROAD
Farringdon Station
Barbican Station
Barbican
ST. LUKE'S

Gray's Inn
Chancery Lane
Farringdon
Smithfield Market
Barbican Centre
Moorgate Station
Moorgate
Liverpool Street Station
Dennis Severs' House
Shoreditch
BRICK LANE
COMMERCIAL STREET

HOLBORN
Holborn
Sir John Soane's Mus.
Museum of London

East London **158**

BISHOPSGATE

Covent Garden to Ludgate Hill **98**

The City **40**

Liverpool Street

Aldgate East
Aldgate

ST. GILES
Royal Courts of Justice
ALDWYCH
City Thameslink
St. Paul's
St. Paul's Cathedral
CITY
Bank of England

Covent Garden
Covent Garden
Temple
Blackfriars
QUEEN VICTORIA ST.
Mansion House
Bank
Mansion House
Fenchurch St. Station
Tower Gateway

STRAND
Temple
Blackfriars Sta.
UPPER THAMES ST.
Cannon Street Station
Monument
TOWER HILL
Tower Hill

Leicester Square
STRAND
EMBANKMENT
BLACKFRIARS BRIDGE
MILLENNIUM BRIDGE
SOUTHWARK BRIDGE
Cannon St.
LONDON BRIDGE

National Gallery
Charing Cross
VICTORIA EMBANKMENT
WATERLOO BRIDGE
Somerset House
Thames
National Theatre
Tate Modern
Shakespeare's Globe
Tower of London

Charing Cross Sta.
JUBILEE BR.
GOLDEN
Embankment
South Bank **70**
Southwark Cathedral
London Br.
TOOLEY
London Bridge Sta.
H.M.S. *Belfast*
City Hall
TOWER BRIDGE

WHITEHALL
Southbank Centre
London Eye
Waterloo
Southwark
Old Operating Theatre
ST. THOMAS ST.
London Bridge Sta.
Butler's Wharf

Ministry of Defence
WESTMINSTER BR.
Waterloo Station
WATERLOO RD.
Dungeon
Borough
LONG LANE
Greenwich

Horse Guards Parade
London Aquarium
Lambeth North
WESTMINSTER BR. RD.
BLACKFRIARS RD.
BOROUGH RD.
SOUTHWARK
GREAT DOVER STREET
TOWER BRIDGE RD.

Big Ben
Westminster Abbey
Houses of Parliament
LAMBETH PALACE RD.
ST. GEORGES RD.
BOROUGH HIGH ST.

WESTMINSTER
LAMBETH BRIDGE
Lambeth Palace
LAMBETH ROAD
Imperial War Museum
NEW KENT ROAD
Elephant & Castle

Tate Britain
MILLBANK
ALBERT EMBANKMENT
KENNINGTON ROAD
LAMBETH
NEWINGTON

VAUXHALL
VAUXHALL BRIDGE
Vauxhall
Vauxhall Station
KENNINGTON LANE
KENNINGTON PARK RD.
Kennington

KENNINGTON ROAD
KENNINGTON PARK RD.
THE OVAL
OVAL
Oval

Covent Garden Flower Market

London

0 ———— 1 mile
0 ———— 1 kilometer

The City

First settled by the Romans around A.D. 50, the oldest part of London is known somewhat confusingly as the City. Covering a little over a square mile (2.6 sq km), with sections of Roman wall still visible, this neighborhood is now a world financial center. Historic buildings, scores of old pubs, and the headquarters of a hundred or so craft guilds, known as livery companies, are located here. Start at the area's highest point, St. Paul's Cathedral, for a view across London from the dome. Admire some of the 47 churches clustered within the square mile, visit Guildhall (the City's ancient seat of government), and explore the Museum of London, the best place to find out about the City's past. On weekdays, the area bustles as 311,000 workers come and go. Evenings and weekends it's quiet—only 10,000 people live here. The buildings may be tightly packed and the main thoroughfares busy, with skyscrapers nudging historic landmarks, but side streets lead to winding medieval lanes, quaint pubs, and leafy churchyards.

❶ **The City's symbol, a griffin holding a shield emblazoned with the Cross of St. George, marks the boundary.**

The City

Nicknamed the Square Mile, the City is easy to get around on foot. Look out for names that describe the trades of old, such as Bread Street and Cloth Fair.

7 Guildhall (see pp. 46–47)
For some 800 years, the Guildhall has been the seat of government for the City. Continue along Gresham Street, then turn right onto Aldersgate Street.

6 Bank of England Museum (see p. 46) Learn all about banking in the capital. Outside, turn left onto Lothbury, which leads onto Gresham Street.

8 Museum of London
(see p. 47) Discover how Londoners have lived from prehistoric times to the 21st century. Outside, turn left onto the Barbican Highwalk.

9 Barbican Centre (see p. 47)
The City's cultural showcase is a large venue that includes the Museum of London as well as performance spaces, two theaters, a concert hall, galleries, and movie theaters.

400 meters
400 yards

CHARTERHOUSE SQUARE

ALDERSGATE STREET

BEECH STREET

CHISWELL STREET

Barbican Centre **9**

Barbican

Museum of London **8**

LONDON WALL

Moorgate Station

FINSBURY PAVEMENT

FINSBURY CIRCUS

MOORGATE

LONDON WALL

GRESHAM Guildhall **7**

MONTAGUE ST.

KING EDWARD

NEWGATE ST.

SHOPSGATE

① St. Paul's Cathedral (see pp. 48–49) Climb to the dome of this monumental church, designed by Sir Christopher Wren, for a fabulous view of London. Behind St. Paul's, cross New Change (past a new shopping mall) onto Watling Street, then turn left onto Queen Victoria Street.

② Temple of Mithras (see p. 44) View the foundations of a third-century Roman temple, then continue up Queen Victoria Street to Mansion House Place.

③ Mansion House (see p. 44) Admire the official home of the Lord Mayor of London, then turn right and walk down King William Street and turn left onto Monument Street.

④ Monument (see p. 45) Climb to the top of this monument to the Great Fire of 1666. Back on ground level, continue on Monument Street, then turn left onto Botolph Street, which becomes Lime Street.

⑤ Lloyd's Building (see p. 45) Crane your neck to view this strikingly modern glass building. Walk around Lloyd's, turn left onto Leadenhall Street, and follow Cornhill to Threadneedle Street.

THE CITY DISTANCE: 5.3 MILES (8.5 KM) TIME: APPROX. 5–7 HOURS
TUBE START: ST. PAUL'S OR MANSION HOUSE

THE CITY

St. Paul's Cathedral

1 See pp. 48–49.

St. Paul's Churchyard, EC4 • www.stpauls.co.uk • 020 7236 4128 • £££
• Sunday: Open for worship only • Tube: St. Paul's or Mansion House

GOOD **EATS**

■ KONDITOR & COOK
Admire one of the City's latest architectural extravaganzas from the café at the foot of the "gherkin" skyscraper. Choose brownies from the spread of desserts or a lunch dish such as spinach pie. **30 St. Mary Axe, EC3, 0845 262 3030, £**

■ LAMB TAVERN
Rub shoulders with City bankers over slow-roasted lamb shanks in a pub that has been in Leadenhall Market since 1780. **10–12 Leadenhall Market, EC3, 020 7626 2454, £££**

■ SWEETINGS
Crab soup, oysters, and smoked eel are usually on the menu in this restaurant, which has changed little in more than a hundred years. **39 Queen Victoria St., EC4, 0844 567 2326, ££**

Temple of Mithras

2 The City stands within the 2-mile-long (3.2 km) wall built by the Romans. Among their legacies are the foundations of a mid-third-century **temple,** discovered in 1954 on Walbrook Street. It was dedicated to Mithras, a Persian god revered by Roman soldiers. The layout resembles that of Christian churches, which it predates. The ruins were moved stone by stone to their present position.

Queen Victoria St. (south side), EC4
• www.visitthecity.co.uk • Tube: Mansion House

Mansion House

3 The Lord Mayor of London and his family live in this sumptuous Georgian palace. The Lord Mayor, who is elected for a one-year term by members of the City of London Corporation, acts as the City's unpaid ambassador both at home and abroad. Built to show off the City's wealth, taste, and power, the **Salon** sparkles with great chandeliers, while the former ballroom and 90-foot-long (27 m) **Great Egyptian Room** hosts conferences and social functions. There is a collection of 17th-century Dutch paintings and a display of gold and silver-plate artifacts, including candelabra, bowls, and flagons, and the Lord Mayor's sword and mace.

Mansion House Place, EC4 • www.cityoflondon.gov.uk • 020 7606 3030 • ££ (tours only: Tues. p.m.; Walbrook entrance) • Closed Aug. and bank holidays • Tube: Bank or Cannon Street

THE CITY

Monument

4 Crowned with a golden flame, this stone Roman Doric column designed by Sir Christopher Wren celebrates the regeneration of the City after the Great Fire of 1666. The fire, which raged for four days and destroyed most of the City's buildings, began in a bakery on Pudding Lane. The Monument stands 202 feet (61 m) tall, and if laid on its side, it would reach the bakery where the conflagration started. A climb up 311 steps leads to the **viewing gallery** and spectacular views over London. Those who cannot make the climb can see a live **webcam panorama** in the lobby.

Monument St., EC3 • www.themonument.info • 020 7626 2717 • £ • Closed: Jan. 1 and Dec. 24–26 • Tube: Monument

Lloyd's Building

5 This 1984 building includes an 84-foot-high (26 m) central atrium. Designed by Richard Rogers, co-architect of the groundbreaking Pompidou Centre in Paris, it is home to Lloyd's of London, the world's leading market for insurers. Two remnants of Lloyd's long history have been relocated to the ultramodern glass skyscraper. The **Adam Room,** designed by the Scottish architect Robert Adam in 1763 as a dining room for the Earl of Shelburne, graces the 11th floor. The centerpiece of the atrium, the **Lutine bell,** was salvaged from the British warship HMS *Lutine* in 1799. At one time, it was rung to announce good and bad news on ships insured by members of Lloyd's. Today it is not used except in times of national or international mourning, such as the death of a member of the royal family.

1 Lime St., EC3 • www.lloyds.com • 020 7327 6586 • £££ (tours for business-related groups only; advance reservation required) • Tube: Monument or Bank

The iconic 1980s Lloyd's Building has glass elevators and other infrastructure exposed to dramatic effect on its exterior.

Bank of England Museum

6 Look up from what appears to be an impenetrable stone bastion at street level to see the great mansion housing the Bank of England above. Its museum, peopled by costumed wax figures, features items stretching back 300 years. These include real and forged banknotes, gold bars, documents, and weights.

Bartholomew Lane, EC2 • www.bankofengland.co.uk/education/museum
• 020 7601 5545 • Closed bank holidays • Tube: Bank

Guildhall

7 For more than 800 years, elected merchants and financiers have held court and laid down the law here. The huge medieval **Great Hall,** built in 1411 and rebuilt after bomb damage in 1941, is still used as a banquet hall. Its windows show the names of London mayors since 1189. Wooden statues of the giants Gog and Magog,

The annual Pearly Kings and Queens Harvest Festival celebrations begin at Guildhall.

mythical founders of the City, are paraded in the annual Lord Mayor's Show (see p. 52). Set around a courtyard, Guildhall includes a **library,** the **Clockmakers' Museum,** and the **Guildhall Art Gallery.** The gallery displays 250 paintings, among which are views of London and works by the Pre-Raphaelites. You can also see what little remains of a **Roman amphitheater** beneath Guildhall Yard.

Gresham St., EC2 • www.guildhall.cityoflondon.gov.uk • 020 7332 1463
• Closed Sun. (except May–Sept.) and for official functions • Tube: Bank or St. Paul's

Museum of London

⑧ This is the place to learn about the capital and its past, from its prehistoric origins as a settlement on the marshy banks of the Thames to the present. Highlights include a gallery devoted to the **Great Fire** of 1666 and the red and gold **Lord Mayor's Coach,** still in use once a year but built more than 250 years ago. The museum shows the lives of Londoners through the ages, using costumes, oral histories, and shop interiors, along with scenes such as the **Victorian Walk.**

150 London Wall, EC2 • www.museumoflondon.org.uk
• 020 7001 9844 • Closed Dec. 24–26 • Tube: Barbican, St. Paul's, or Moorgate

SAVVY **TRAVELER**

For a glimpse of how London's landmarks looked in the past, download Streetmuseum, a mobile phone app from the Museum of London that matches historic photographs to your location.

Barbican Centre

⑨ Constructed in the 1970s on a site bombed in World War II, the Barbican Centre is part of a larger residential complex named for a long-lost city fortification. The **Lakeside Terrace** provides a tranquil place to relax in the heart of the City. Inside the building, two theaters, a concert hall (home of the **London Symphony Orchestra**), two art galleries, and three movie theaters hum with activity.

Silk St., EC2 • www.barbican.org.uk • 020 7638 4141; box office: 020 7638 8891
• £££–£££££ • Tube: Barbican or Moorgate

St. Paul's Cathedral

The crowning glory of the City, this domed cathedral church took
35 years to complete and is an architectural masterpiece.

Pale Portland stone was transported by boat from Dorset for the construction of St. Paul's.

London's Anglican cathedral, the first to be built for the English Protestant faith, is a marvel of architectural engineering and a fitting monument to the genius of its architect, Sir Christopher Wren. After the Great Fire of London destroyed its more conventional predecessor in 1666, Wren was left to devise an entirely new building in the style of his own time—English baroque. The result, completed in 1710, is a majestic space of marble and mosaics, soaring to a triumphant dome.

■ CELEBRATIONS & MEMORIALS

From the top of Ludgate Hill, the front of St. Paul's Cathedral is an imposing sight, its steps leading up to the 30-foot-high (9 m) **Great West Door.** Used for ceremonial occasions, such as the 1981 wedding of Lady Diana Spencer to Prince Charles, St. Paul's contains monuments to national heroes, including the **Duke of Wellington** (in the nave) and **Admiral Lord Nelson** (in the South Transept).

■ EXQUISITE EMBELLISHMENTS

The church is built in the shape of a cross. Ceiling mosaics were added after Queen Victoria described the building as "dreary, dingy and undevotional." The **choir stalls** were decorated by Britain's best-known wood carver, the 18th-century master Grinling Gibbons, and the magnificent gilded **wrought-iron work** throughout the cathedral is by a French master metalworker, Jean Tijou. The **high altar** was made in 1958, with a canopy based on a sketch by Wren. Also in 1958, the **American Memorial Chapel** behind the altar was opened, with a roll of honor to the 28,000 Americans who died in the defense of Europe during World War II.

■ THE DOME

At 365 feet (111 m) high, the dome is almost as tall as St. Peter's Basilica in Vatican City. The first stop after climbing 257 spiraling steps is the **Whispering Gallery,** so called because if you whisper something while facing the wall, someone on the opposite side of the gallery, 105 feet (32 m) away, can hear you clearly. From here you can see the paintings of St. Paul by James Thornhill that decorate the dome. Climb another 271 steps to the external **Golden Gallery** for views across London.

■ THE CRYPT

The **Duke of Wellington** and **Admiral Lord Nelson,** Napoleon's vanquishers, are both entombed in the crypt. Many well-known names are honored here, including Wren himself. His epitaph ends: "Reader, if you seek his monument, look around you."

SAVVY **TRAVELER**

The crypt contains a good café serving hot and cold food, a restaurant, and an area to sit and relax. The entrance is on the north side of the church, and you don't need a ticket to visit.

St. Paul's Churchyard, EC4 • www.stpauls.co.uk • 020 7236 4128 • £££ • Sun.: Open for worship only, free • Tube: St. Paul's or Mansion House

Wren Churches

Within the square mile that defines the City of London an exceptional group of churches chart the evolving story of ecclesiastical architecture in England. Some survive from medieval times, but most are linked with Sir Christopher Wren, the scientist turned architect responsible for rebuilding 51 of the 80 churches destroyed in the Great Fire of 1666. Many, restored after being damaged in World War II, have modern elements.

Sir Christopher Wren appears in a stained-glass window in St. Lawrence Jewry (above); Wren rebuilt St. Mary-le-Bow (right) over the crypt of an 11th-century church.

Inventive Designs

Rising from the ashes of the Great Fire, Sir Christopher Wren's churches represented an innovative style that suited the new Protestant way of worship of the time. Central to his design was an interior where, in his words, the congregation could "hear distinctly and see the preacher."

Classical Look

Construction work on **St. Mary-le-Bow** (*Cheapside, EC2, www.stmarylebow.co.uk, 020 7248 5139, closed Sat.–Sun.*), one of the first churches to be rebuilt, began just two years after the fire. Wren's classical 224-foot-high (68 m) steeple set the standard for other architects. (Londoners have a special affection for this church since only those born within the sound of Bow bells are said to be true Cockneys.)

One of the most splendid of the Wren churches is **St. Mary Abchurch** (*Abchurch La., EC4, www.london-city-churches.org.uk, 020 7626 0306, closed Wed. and Sat.–Sun.*). Completed in 1686, it reveals Wren's genius for turning a small space into a thing

THE CITY

of splendor. The dome over the nave is invisible from the outside, giving an effect described by the poet John Betjeman as "both uplifting and intimate." Among its other glories is a reredos by Grinling Gibbons, the wood-carver who worked on St. Paul's Cathedral (see pp. 48–49).

Prototype Dome

St. Stephen Walbrook *(Walbrook, EC4, www.ststephenwalbrook.net, 020 7626 9000, closed Sat.–Sun.)* was the first domed church in Britain. It would have had special meaning for Wren as his own parish church—he lived at No. 15 Walbrook. The ornate dome, supported by eight Corinthian pillars and arches, acted as a prototype for St. Paul's.

The Guild Church of the Corporation of London, **St. Lawrence Jewry** *(Gresham St., EC2, www.london-city-churches.org .uk, 020 7626 1555, closed Sat.– Sun.)*, on Gresham Street, stands near Guildhall (see pp. 46–47). See the stained-glass windows in the vestibule depicting Wren, Gibbons, and master mason Edward Strong, the men who created these churches.

Celebrations

Throughout the year, musicians, dancers, and performance artists take to the streets and parks, and competing crews head out onto the River Thames itself for an annual round of festivals and events. Some events celebrate modern London's diverse ethnic mix; others are decades or even centuries old.

■ LORD MAYOR'S SHOW

The Lord Mayor's Show harkens back almost 800 years to the days of King John, when the newly elected Lord Mayor traveled from the City to Westminster to pledge his allegiance to the Crown. On a Saturday each November, marching bands, floats, musicians, and dancers start at Guildhall, then pass St. Paul's on their way to the Royal Courts of Justice, where the Lord Mayor takes the oath of allegiance. The day ends with fireworks over the Thames at 5 p.m.

www.lordmayorsshow.org • Nov.
• Tube: Bank, St. Paul's, or Temple

■ THAMES FESTIVAL

This free outdoor festival over a weekend in September celebrates the best arts and music the capital has to offer. Stage performances, art installations, bands, dancing, and food stalls take over the banks of the Thames from Westminster to Tower Bridge, culminating in a night carnival and fantastic fireworks display.

www.thamesfestival.org • Sept. • Tube: Waterloo, Embankment, London Bridge, or Tower Hill

■ NEW YEAR'S DAY PARADE & FESTIVAL

Marching bands, dancers, and street performers parade through Piccadilly Circus, Trafalgar Square, and Whitehall to Parliament Street on New Year's Day.

www.londonparade.co.uk • Jan. 1
• Tube: Piccadilly Circus or Charing Cross

■ CHINESE NEW YEAR

Celebrations are held on the weekend after Chinese New Year (a lunar festival, Chinese New Year is on a different date each year). Enjoy colorful lion dances, acrobats, parading dragons, and food stalls in and around Gerrard Street, or

Traditionally, Watermen took the Lord Mayor by barge to take his oath; today they go on foot.

go to Trafalgar Square to hear Chinese music and dance on a giant stage.

www.chinatownlondon.org • Jan. or Feb.
• Tube: Leicester Square

■ THE NOTTING HILL CARNIVAL
Europe's largest street event celebrates the dynamic and diverse Afro-Caribbean community in London. Held on the last weekend in August, the three-day street party begins on Saturday, when steel bands compete for the title "Champions of Steel." Sunday is the Kids' Carnival and Monday the carnival parade. Expect huge crowds, flamboyant costumes,

lavish floats, loud reggae and calypso music, and thousands of performers.

www.thenottinghillcarnival.com • Aug.
• Tube: Notting Hill Gate or Ladbroke Grove

■ THE BOAT RACE
Begun in 1829, this annual race is part of the rivalry between the universities of Oxford and Cambridge. Eight-man boats row the 4-mile (6.4 km) course in west London from Putney Bridge to Chiswick Bridge. Join the cheering spectators on the riverbank, or watch the race from a waterside pub.

www.theboatrace.org • March or April
• Tube: Hammersmith or Putney Bridge

Westminster

All the pomp and ceremony of London is centered around Westminster, perched on the north bank of the Thames and bounded by Hyde Park to the west and Regent Street to the east. Stand in Parliament Square to see the twin pillars of the British establishment: Westminster Abbey, where kings and queens are crowned, and the Palace of Westminster, better known as the Houses of Parliament, where elected governments come and go. Through the trees in nearby St. James's Park you can see Buckingham Palace. On special occasions, members of the royal family appear on the palace balcony. Heading north from Parliament Square, the wide avenue of Whitehall passes near the subterranean Churchill War Rooms. On the west side of Whitehall, Horse Guards Parade provides a grand setting for royal ceremonies such as Trooping the Colour. Away from the politics and pageantry, great art collections vie for attention with some of London's smartest shops and swankiest restaurants in the elegant surroundings of Piccadilly and Mayfair.

◀ **Westminster Abbey's massive, soaring West Towers, added in the 18th century, were designed by architect Nicholas Hawksmoor.**

NEIGHBORHOOD **WALK**

7 Handel House Museum
(see p. 62) See exhibits relating to George Frideric Handel's life and work. Continue on Brook Street, then turn right onto Duke Street.

8 Wallace Collection (see pp. 62–63) Enjoy the fine collection of European paintings, furniture, and decorative art. Retrace your steps to Oxford Street, and walk west through throngs of shoppers toward Hyde Park.

9 Marble Arch (see p. 63) The former gateway to Buckingham Palace now stands in splendid isolation at the west end of Oxford Street. Head south down Park Lane, then left onto Curzon Street and Shepherd Market.

10 Shepherd Market
(see p. 63) An eclectic mix of pubs, restaurants, and boutiques fills the narrow streets of this lively part of Mayfair.

1 Buckingham Palace (see p. 58) Start at the Queen's London home for the daily ceremony of Changing the Guard. Explore the Queen's Gallery and Royal Mews. Then go along the south side of St. James's Park on Birdcage Walk to Parliament Square.

WESTMINSTER

WESTMINSTER DISTANCE: 4 MILES (6.4 KM) TIME: APPROX. 8 HOURS
TUBE START: HYDE PARK CORNER, GREEN PARK, OR VICTORIA

Westminster

Some of the nation's best known buildings cluster in this one corner of London.

6 Royal Academy of Arts (see p. 61) View the small permanent collection or see a blockbuster visiting exhibit before heading north again along Old Bond Street and left onto Brook Street to the Handel House Museum.

5 Horse Guards (see pp. 60–61) Leave the headquarters of the Household Cavalry, and with St. James's Park on your left, head north to Piccadilly to the Royal Academy of Arts.

4 Churchill War Rooms (see p. 60) Visit Churchill's World War II bunker, then go up Whitehall to Horse Guards Parade.

3 Houses of Parliament (see pp. 58–59) Once you have seen the "mother of parliaments" and listened to Big Ben striking the hour, stop to admire the view from Westminster Bridge, then cross Parliament Square to Great George Street.

2 Westminster Abbey (see pp. 64–65) See where monarchs have been crowned and buried for nearly a thousand years, then go along the side of Parliament Square and cross St. Margaret Street to the Houses of Parliament.

Map labels:
REGENT STREET
Charing Cross
COCKSPUR ST. NORTHUMBERLAND AVE.
ST. JAMES'S SQUARE
PALL MALL
ST. JAMES'S
THE MALL
WHITEHALL
HORSE GUARDS ROAD
5 Horse Guards
ST. JAMES'S PARK
DUCK ISLAND
Banqueting House
St. James's Park Lake
4 Churchill War Rooms
GREAT GEORGE ST.
BIRDCAGE WALK
Westminster
WESTMINSTER BRIDGE
PARLIAMENT SQUARE
Westminster Abbey
2
3 Houses of Parliament
Thames
St. James's Park
VICTORIA STREET
GREAT SMITH ST.
WESTMINSTER
0   400 meters
0   400 yards

Buckingham Palace

1 Old Master paintings, furniture, and porcelain from the Royal Collection decorate Buckingham Palace's 19 **State Rooms,** which open to the public each August–September. A visit to this 775-room mansion is otherwise rewarded by the sight of changing guards (see p. 67) or even a glimpse of a member of the royal family swooping past in the back of a limousine. See the new guard marching to the palace from Wellington Barracks, to the left of the palace as you face it, each morning. **St. James's Park** is a good viewing point. On the south side of the Palace, the **Queen's Gallery** houses changing exhibitions of works from the Royal Collection, which was acquired by the present Queen's predecessors more than 400 years ago and is held in trust by her for the nation. Just beyond the gallery are the **Royal Mews,** home to the Windsor Grey horses that draw the Queen's carriage. The Gold State Coach used for coronations and other grand state occasions, seven other historic carriages used for ceremonial occasions, and the gold-braided state livery worn by coachmen and equerries show how the royals travel.

The Mall, SW1 • www.royalcollection.org.uk • State Rooms: 020 7766 7300, £££££, open Aug.–Sept. (dates change yearly), exclusive tours (£££££) can be booked outside the summer opening season • Queen's Gallery: £££, closed public holidays • Royal Mews: £££, opening times vary through the year • Tube: Hyde Park Corner, Green Park, or Victoria

Westminster Abbey

2 See pp. 64–65.

Broad Sanctuary, SW1 • www.westminster-abbey.org • 020 7222 5152 • £££££ • Sun.: Open for worship only, free • Tube: Westminster

Houses of Parliament

3 Opposite Westminster Abbey stands the familiar Victorian, neo-Gothic Palace of Westminster, built after fire destroyed its predecessor in 1834. Listen for **Big Ben,** which strikes every hour, with four smaller bells striking the quarters, from the **clock tower**

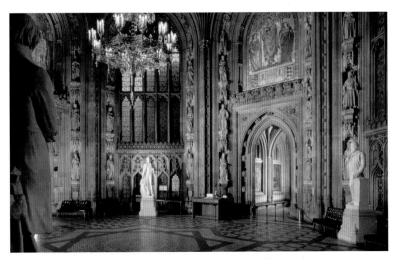
Statues of kings and queens fill the Central Lobby of the Houses of Parliament.

at the building's northern end. At its southern end is the **Victoria Tower,** which was the tallest secular structure in the world when it was completed in 1858. The Queen uses the Sovereign's Entrance at the base of the tower whenever she visits the building. Visitors, who can attend debates and watch committees when Parliament is in session, use St. Stephen's entrance on Parliament Square, which leads to the **Central Lobby.** They can also climb the **Central Tower** above the lobby. The **House of Lords,** the upper chamber, is off to the right of the lobby. To the left of the lobby is the **House of Commons,** the chamber where elected Members of Parliament (MPs) sit. On the left of St. Stephen's entrance is the **Great Hall,** the historic heart of the building. Dating from 1097, it has the largest timber roof in northern Europe, and beneath its ancient beams countless laws have been passed, trials held, and coronation breakfasts eaten.

Parliament Square, SW1 • www.parliament.uk • 0844 847 1672 • Tube: Westminster

Churchill War Rooms

4 During World War II, Sir Winston Churchill and his cabinet directed military operations from an underground bunker between Parliament Square and the Prime Minister's residence at 10 Downing Street. Churchill had his own room with a desk and bed, although he slept there on only three occasions. He delivered some of his major wartime speeches from the desk in 1940, as London

came under ferocious bombardment. Beside the bed is an ashtray, creating a lingering feeling that Churchill, smoking one of his famous cigars, has just left the room. The other rooms are preserved much as they were at the height of the conflict. In the **Cabinet Room,** the chiefs of staff made decisions, and in the **Map Room,** Army, Navy, and Air Force officers notched up the scores of planes shot down in the Battle of Britain and followed the ebb and flow of numerous other battles. Churchill kept in touch with the White House from the **transatlantic telephone room,** converted from a broom closet.

The Map Room—its walls covered with maps, charts, and notes— was the hub of Churchill's World War II bunker.

King Charles St., SW1 • http://cwr.iwm.org.uk • 020 7930 6961 • ££££££ • Closed Dec. 24–26 • Tube: Westminster or St. James's Park

Horse Guards

5 Farther up Whitehall toward Trafalgar Square, past Downing Street, this ensemble of buildings replaced the former Palace of Whitehall, which burned down in the 1690s. Today Horse Guards is famous for the mounted soldiers from the Household Cavalry who stand guard in plumed hats and thigh-high boots, swords drawn. Two are on duty each day from 10 a.m. to 4 p.m. The old palace's jousting yard is now **Horse Guards Parade,** an open space used for ceremonies such as the Queen's annual birthday parade in June, better known as **Trooping the Colour** (see p. 67).

The Household Cavalry mounts the guard at Horse Guards between 10 a.m and 4 p.m., and the guard changes at 11 a.m. A Dismounting Ceremony takes place at 4 p.m. You can also see the troopers tending their horses in the 18th-century stables that are part of the **Household Cavalry Museum.** Here, you can find out about the two Household Cavalry regiments, which have provided an escort for the monarch for 350 years and also continue to serve queen and country in conflicts around the world.

Whitehall, SW1 • www.householdcavalrymuseum.co.uk • 020 7930 3070 • ££ • Closed Dec. 24–26 • Tube: Westminster or Piccadilly Circus

Royal Academy of Arts

6 Privately funded and independently run, the Royal Academy on Piccadilly is Britain's premier artists' society. It occupies **Burlington House,** the last remaining 17th-century noble mansion on Piccadilly, on the far side of a large fountain-filled courtyard that it shares with several other venerable institutions. Free tours of the **John Madejski Fine Rooms** provide a background to the workings of the Academy, with pictures from its collection on view. Major international loan exhibitions are put on throughout the year, but the highlight is the **Summer Exhibition,** an annual show of paintings, prints, and sculpture by Academicians and members of the public. Anyone can submit work for consideration by the hanging committee, and successful applicants have the thrill of seeing their creations on show near that of Academicians such as David Hockney and Tracey Emin.

Piccadilly, W1 • www.royalacademy.org.uk • 020 7300 8000 • Loan exhibitions: £££ • Tube: Piccadilly Circus or Green Park

GOOD **EATS**

■ INN THE PARK
A delightful setting by the lake in St. James's Park makes this a good stopping-off point for coffee and ice cream.
Ivy Lodge, St. James's Park, SW1, 020 7451 9999, ££

■ SKETCH PARLOUR CAFE
Louis XV décor goes with the wonderful cakes and pastries of the inviting café in this complex that turns into a nighttime club. The Lecture Room and Library restaurant has a Michelin star.
9 Conduit St., W1, 020 7659 4500, £££

■ THE WOLSELEY
Both opulent and elegant, this former marble-floored car showroom built in the 1920s serves delicious lunches.
160 Piccadilly, W1, 020 7499 6996, ££

WESTMINSTER

Handel House Museum

7 At the southern end of South Moulton Street is the house where George Frideric Handel lived and worked from 1723 until his death in 1759. Handel wrote some of his best-loved compositions here, including the *Messiah* and the *Music for the Royal Fireworks.* The lovingly restored Georgian interiors house a collection of letters, prints, and early editions of operas and oratorios. Visiting ensembles give weekly concerts of baroque music.

25 Brook St., W1 • www.handelhouse.org • 020 7495 1685 • ££ • Closed Mon. and some public holidays • Tube: Bond Street

The Wallace Collection

8 This elegant building and art collection on Manchester Square seem far removed from the busy shops of nearby Oxford Street. The first Marquess of Hertford began the collection in the 18th century

The Wallace Collection holds more than 500 pieces of French porcelain and furniture.

WESTMINSTER

with portraits of his children by Sir Joshua Reynolds and six paintings by the Venetian painter, Canaletto. Paintings from such masters as Rembrandt, Titian, and Velázquez grace the walls. Fragonard's "The Swing" and Poussin's "Dance to the Music of Time" stand out among the many French paintings. Other treasures include furniture by the 18th-century French cabinetmaker André-Charles Boulle and the finest collection of arms and armor in the United Kingdom.

Manchester Square, W1 • www.wallacecollection.org • 020 7563 9500 • Closed Dec. 24–26 • Tube: Bond Street or Marble Arch

Marble Arch

9 Isolated on a traffic island where Oxford Street and Park Lane meet, this triumphal arch was originally built as an entrance to Buckingham Palace and moved here in 1851. Made of Carrera marble and based on the ancient Roman triumphal arch of the emperor Constantine, the arch serves no useful purpose, although it was once used as a police station: From here, officers could keep an eye on **Speaker's Corner** in nearby Hyde Park, a place where anyone can stand up and say what they like. Marble Arch also marks the location of the old Tyburn Tree, site of public hangings until 1783.

Intersection of Oxford St. and Park Lane • Tube: Marble Arch

IN **THE KNOW**

The route from Newgate Prison to the Tyburn gallows followed the route that Oxford Street does now and was known as Tyburn Way. Stalls were set up to serve the crowds who came to watch the hangings.

WESTMINSTER

Shepherd Market

10 Just off Curzon Street, village-like Shepherd Market is an ancient corner of Mayfair (toward its western side) whose small streets are lined with 18th-century houses. This area was the site of the May Fair, an annual fortnight of revelry, banned in 1708, that gave the area its name. Shepherd Market has small, mostly high-end shops and restaurants and several Victorian pubs.

Between Curzon St. and Piccadilly • Tube: Hyde Park Corner or Green Park

Westminster Abbey

*This glorious building sums up all the
pageantry of English history.*

The Choir of Westminster Abbey performs in front of the 19th-century choir screen in the nave.

London's most beautiful building is also its oldest, dating back to a monastery founded in A.D. 960 by 12 Benedictine monks on the banks of the Thames. In the 11th century, King Edward the Confessor built a new, larger abbey and monastery. This, in turn, was replaced by the present Gothic building, started by King Henry III in 1245. Some buildings from Edward's monastery still survive, including parts of nearby Westminster School. The abbey Choir School's 30 boys take part in the daily choral services.

■ HIGH ALTAR

From the north entrance, walk ahead and look to the left to see the high altar above a colorful mosaic pavement from 1268. Behind the altar, **St. Edward's Chapel** commemorates King Edward the Confessor, whose newly built abbey was consecrated in 1065, a year before his death, and who was canonized in 1161. The chapel contains Edward's shrine and the tombs of several other monarchs. Outside the chapel, the high-backed, solid oak **Coronation Chair** rests on four gilt lions. Since 1308, all but two monarchs (King Edward V and King Edward VIII) have been crowned in it.

■ HENRY VII'S LADY CHAPEL

Beyond the Coronation Chair, visit the jewel-like Henry VII's Lady Chapel: Its elegant fan vaulting has the delicacy of lace. Henry belonged to the House of Tudor, whose emblem graces the bronze gates. The king's tomb, together with that of his wife, Elizabeth of York, lies behind the altar. In the **north aisle** of the Lady Chapel you can find the colorful Tudor tombs of Queen Elizabeth I and her half-sister, Queen Mary. Sworn enemies divided by religion in life, here they are united in death. Several other monarchs

SAVVY **TRAVELER**

For a view over the abbey, visit the roof terrace of **Central Hall Westminster** (*Storey's Gate, SW1 www.c-h-w.com 020 7222 8010*), a conference center and Methodist church on Parliament Square.

are entombed in the **south aisle,** including King George II, the last king to be buried in the abbey (in 1760).

■ POETS' CORNER

In the **South Transept,** this area celebrates the lives of English writers. Shakespeare and Lord Byron have monuments, and several others, including Dr. Samuel Johnson and Charles Dickens, are buried here, as is composer George Frideric Handel. The ashes of actor Sir Laurence Olivier are also interred here.

■ NAVE

One hundred and fifty years in the building, the 102-foot-high (31 m) nave is the tallest in England. Among those buried here are Charles Darwin, author of *On the Origin of Species*. Beneath the west window is the tomb of the **Unknown Warrior**, representing all those who died fighting in World War I.

WESTMINSTER

Broad Sanctuary, SW1 • www.westminster-abbey.org • 020 7222 5152 • ££££ • Sunday: Open for worship only • Tube: Westminster

Royal City

Since the days of the Anglo-Saxon king Edward the Confessor, monarchs have added grandeur and glamour to London, choosing it for their power base, shaping its appearance with lavish palaces, and providing scenes of spectacle and pageantry. Royal palaces are rich in history and tradition, and several provide the setting for colorful and spectacular ceremonies whose origins lie deep in the past.

WESTMINSTER

Prince William and Kate Middleton (above) wed in April 2011 in Westminster Abbey; the Tower of London's White Tower (right) was completed in 1097.

Center of Government

When William the Conqueror invaded England in 1066, Winchester in Hampshire was the country's capital. London, however, was the largest city, and William knew he must control it. He chose Edward the Confessor's newly finished **Westminster Abbey** (see pp. 64–65) for his coronation and built the White Tower, the central feature of the **Tower of London** (see pp. 168–169).

In the 12th century, the first Palace of Westminster, to which King William II had added the **Great Hall** (see p. 59), became the main royal residence in London.

Succession of Palaces

In the 16th century, King Henry VIII made the Palace of Whitehall his principal residence. Previously known as York House, it had belonged to Cardinal Wolsey. Henry renamed and extended Whitehall and added a jousting yard—now the site of Horse Guards Parade. In 1622, King James I added **Banqueting House** (*Whitehall SW1, www*

.hrp.org.uk, 020 3166 6154/5, ££, closed Sun., public holidays and Dec. 24–Jan. 1), built to a design by Inigo Jones, who also built the **Queen's House** at Greenwich (see p. 167). Banqueting House has a ceiling painting by Peter Paul Rubens, commissioned by King Charles I, which survived intact when a fire destroyed the rest of Whitehall Palace in 1698.

Less than a mile (1 km) from Banqueting House, the northern gatehouse of **St. James's Palace** (*www.royal.gov.uk*) is one of central London's few Tudor landmarks. King Henry VIII constructed the palace in the 1530s and used it mainly for receiving royal envoys. Even now, ambassadors to the United Kingdom are accredited to the Court of St. James.

In 1761, King George III bought Buckingham House, and in 1828 King George IV asked architect John Nash to transform it into a palace. When Victoria became queen in 1837, the work was unfinished. She moved in nevertheless, and **Buckingham Palace** (see p. 58) has been the official London royal residence ever since.

ROYAL **CEREMONIES**

Changing the Guard
Each morning, the guard at Buckingham Palace is replaced. **Buckingham Palace (see p. 58), www.changing-the-guard.co.uk, daily 11:30 a.m.–noon**

Trooping the Colour The Foot Guards celebrate the Queen's official birthday by trooping their regimental flag through the ranks. **Horse Guards Parade (see pp. 60–61), www.trooping-the-colour.co.uk, a Sat. in June**

Ceremony of the Keys The Tower of London's gates are locked for the night. **Tower of London (see pp. 168–169), www.hrp.org.uk, nightly**

Beating Retreat A member of the royal family takes the salute. **Horse Guards Parade (see pp. 60–61), www.guards beatingretreat.com, two evenings in June**

WESTMINSTER

Mayfair's Posh Shops

Mayfair, in the northern reaches of Westminster, offers the choicest in upmarket specialty stores, many of which have been operating for hundreds of years. Whether your fancy is window-shopping or splurging on treats, here you will find the perfect jewel, artwork, or handmade truffle.

■ BOND STREET
Short in distance—a mere half-mile (1 km) long—Bond Street offers a heady shopping experience. In addition to the flagship outlets of major fashion designers, including relative newcomer **Christian Dior** (*No. 160*), you'll find jewelers and antique dealers. Diamonds sparkle in the windows of **De Beers** (*No. 50*), and **Asprey** (*No. 167*) sells luggage and accessories as well as jewelry. View an auction at **Bonhams** (*No. 101*) or **Sotheby's** (*Nos. 34–35*), or drop into a high-end gallery such as **Richard Green** (*No. 147*) or the **Fine Art Society** (*No. 148*).

www.bondstreetassociation.com

■ CORK STREET
More art awaits in Cork Street's elegant, long-established galleries east of Bond Street. **Bernard Jacobson** (*No. 6*) is known for the work of Howard Hodgkin, Ben Nicholson, and Helen Frankenthaler.

Redfern (*No. 20*) represents more than 20 contemporary artists and their estates, among them Patrick Procktor and the sculptor Lisa Lombardi. Stop at **Flowers** (*No. 21*), where you might spot a John Kirby print or Jiro Osuga painting, while **Adam Gallery** (*No. 24*) has a roster of major artists from the early 20th century onward, including Georges Braque and Patrick Heron.

www.galleries.co.uk/g-crk.htm

■ BURLINGTON ARCADE
Just south of Cork Street, this glass-roofed shopping avenue twinkles with antique silver, jewelry, and high-end watches. Opened in 1819, it was Britain's first shopping arcade and remains a treasure trove of specialist stores. Pop into **N. Peal** (*Nos. 37–40*) for cashmere sweaters, **Pickett** (*Nos. 32–33 & 40*) for English-made leather goods, and **Globe-Trotter** (*Nos. 54–55*) for luxury luggage made by a secret

WESTMINSTER

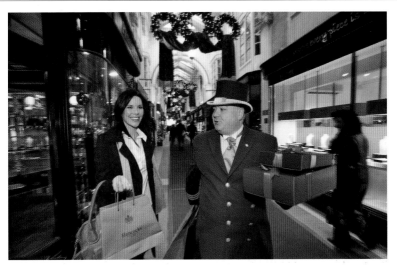

Shop for luxury treats in elegant surroundings at Burlington Arcade.

method. Guards in top hats patrol the arcade on the lookout for such unruly behavior as whistling and running.

www.burlington-arcade.co.uk

■ SAVILE ROW

The world's premier street for custom-made gentlemen's tailoring is lined with Georgian buildings where perfect suits are lovingly crafted. **Gieves and Hawkes** (*No. 1*), tailors since 1771, dressed the explorer Robert Scott and writer Noel Coward. Or you can follow in the footsteps of style icons Fred Astaire and Marlene Dietrich and visit **Anderson & Sheppard**, around the corner on Old Burlington Street (*No. 32*). The daddy of them all is **Henry Poole & Co.** (*No. 15*), the first tailor to set up shop in "The Row" in 1822. Charles Dickens and Napoleon III were customers.

www.savilerowbespoke.com

■ FORTNUM & MASON

The finest grocery store in the neighborhood sells wines produced only for Fortnum's and honey from its rooftop apiary. Treat yourself to a pot of Fortnum Pickle or a packet of Chocolossus Biscuits. Then relax over afternoon tea.

181 Piccadilly, W1 • www.fortnumand mason.com • 020 7734 8040

SOUTH
BANK

South Bank

Soar above the city on the stratospheric wheel of the London Eye, then stroll from Westminster Bridge to Tower Bridge to enjoy a nearly limitless supply of free entertainment. Attend a festival, listen to live music, jog, cycle, skateboard, or simply walk along the 3-mile (4.8 km) riverfront. Step into the free Tate Modern art gallery, worth visiting as much for the architecture and the views from the cafe as for the art inside. Paying attractions include a cluster of cultural centers around Waterloo Bridge, housing the Southbank Centre's concert halls, the National Theatre, and the British Film Institute. Travel back in time at the rebuilt Globe theater, where you can see plays performed as they were in Shakespeare's time. Continue east, stopping to admire a replica of the ship that took Sir Francis Drake around the world. Nearby Clink Prison is not for the fainthearted. Foodies will find delights aplenty at Borough Market's al fresco stalls, while the restaurants of Butler's Wharf just east of Tower Bridge serve up pricier fare in more formal surroundings.

❍ **Traveling at a gentle speed of about 10 inches (25 cm) per second, the London Eye carries you far above the capital.**

South Bank

Promenade along this section of the Thames to catch the best river views.
Stop for lunch or a snack, then take in an art show or concert.

❹ **National Theatre**
(see p. 75) In summer
catch a performance in
front of the building,
then stroll east toward
the Millennium Bridge.

❺ **Tate Modern** (see
pp. 78–79) Art created since
1900 occupies this former
power station. Continue east
alongside the river.

❸ **Southbank Centre**
(see pp. 74–75) Visit London's
leading arts center for an art show
or a performance before continuing
on under Waterloo Bridge.

SOUTH BANK

❷ **London Eye** (see p. 74)
Float upward on this giant
wheel for the best views
of the city. Next, walk
northeast along the river
for about five minutes.

❶ **Imperial War
Museum** (see p. 74) After
exploring the collection
of arms and weapons,
head northwest toward
Westminster Bridge, then
take the steps on the right
just before the bridge.

SOUTHBANK   DISTANCE: 3.5 MILES (5.4 KM)
TIME: APPROX. 4–6 HOURS   TUBE START: LAMBETH NORTH

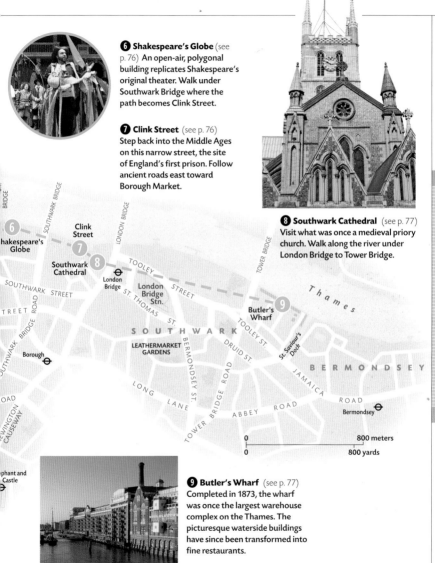

❻ Shakespeare's Globe (see p. 76) An open-air, polygonal building replicates Shakespeare's original theater. Walk under Southwark Bridge where the path becomes Clink Street.

❼ Clink Street (see p. 76) Step back into the Middle Ages on this narrow street, the site of England's first prison. Follow ancient roads east toward Borough Market.

❽ Southwark Cathedral (see p. 77) Visit what was once a medieval priory church. Walk along the river under London Bridge to Tower Bridge.

❾ Butler's Wharf (see p. 77) Completed in 1873, the wharf was once the largest warehouse complex on the Thames. The picturesque waterside buildings have since been transformed into fine restaurants.

Imperial War Museum

1 Large weapons, tanks, and fighter aircraft vie for the visitor's attention, but it is exhibits such as the re-creation of a **trench** from World War I and the sights, sounds, and smells of the World War II **Blitz Experience** that are the most popular, capturing the reality of war for soldiers and ordinary people. Diaries, photo albums, and toys are among the moving items used to illustrate the Holocaust. War art includes works by Paul Nash and Henry Moore.

Lambeth Road, SE1 • www.iwm.org.uk • 020 7416 5000 • Closed Dec. 24–26 • Tube: Lambeth North

SAVVY **TRAVELER**

Book a "flight" on the London Eye online to get a discount and avoid the lines, which can be lengthy, especially in summer. The ticket office is next to the London Eye, in County Hall, former home of London's local government. County Hall now also houses **Namco Station,** a palace of games, bumper cars, and bowling. The **Sea Life London Aquarium** is here, too, showing marine life over three floors, including tanks for some 40 sharks.

London Eye

2 Adding its own distinctive silhouette to the London skyline, the Eye, at 443 feet (135 m) high, is the world's tallest cantilevered observation wheel. The gentle ascent in one of its pods reveals glorious views across the capital, from the Houses of Parliament, almost below, in a 25-mile (40 km) sweep south to the North Downs hills, east to Elizabeth II Bridge, and west to Windsor Castle.

Riverside Building, County Hall, Westminster Bridge, SE1 • www.londoneye.com • 0870 990 8883 • £££ • Closed Dec. 25 • Tube: Waterloo, Embankment, or Westminster

Southbank Centre

3 At the heart of the South Bank's buzzing arts complex lies the **Royal Festival Hall,** which opened in 1951 as part of the Festival of Britain to bolster spirits (and business) after World War II. It is home to four resident orchestras, including the London Philharmonic and London Sinfonietta, while smaller ensembles perform at the adjacent **Queen Elizabeth Hall** and **Purcell Room.** The Festival Hall's main bar and **Clore Ballroom** often offer free live music, while the riverside terrace is ideal for people-watching. The **Hayward Gallery**

Airplanes at the Imperial War Museum include a Sopwith Camel, center, and a Spitfire, top left.

hosts contemporary art shows, and children will love the cartoons on touch-sensitive monitors in the **Waterloo Sunset Pavilion.** The neighboring **BFI Southbank** screens movies old and new and runs film festivals. Its IMAX cinema has the largest screen in the UK.

South Bank, SE1 • www.southbankcentre.co.uk • 0844 875 0073 • *££–£££££* • Tube: Embankment or Waterloo

National Theatre

4 Opened in 1976, the "NT" stages more than a thousand performances of classical and contemporary drama annually in its three theaters. You can also attend talks, take backstage tours, listen to live music in the foyers, and enjoy the convivial atmosphere—and great views of the river from the terraces—over a drink or dinner.

South Bank, SE1 • www.nationaltheatre.org.uk • 020 7452 3000 • *££–£££££* • Box Office closed public holidays • Tube: Embankment or Waterloo

Tate Modern

5

See pp. 78–79.

Bankside, SE1 • www.tate.org.uk/modern • 020 7887 8888 • Closed Dec. 24–26 • Tube: Southwark, London Bridge, St. Paul's, or Mansion House

Shakespeare's Globe

6

This wonderful reconstruction of William Shakespeare's open-air theater transports visitors back to the turn of the 17th century. Audiences see the play as a late-Elizabethan audience would have, either seated or as "groundlings," standing around the stage. The season starts on Shakespeare's birthday (April 23). Enjoy the space year-round with a tour and a visit to the permanent exhibition, which explains how the building was constructed in the 1990s.

21 New Globe Walk, SE1 • www.shakespearesglobe.com • 020 7902 1400 • Performances daily Apr. 23–early Oct. • Tube: London Bridge

Clink Street

7

Clink Street runs between the riverside Anchor Pub and **St. Mary Overie's Dock,** where you can see a full-scale working replica of Sir Francis Drake's ship, *The Golden Hinde,* in which he circumnavigated the globe in 1577–1580. This narrow street is named for England's first prison, set up in a cellar of the Bishop of Winchester's Palace in 1150. You can still see the west wall and rose window of the palace's Great Hall from the street. **The Clink Prison Museum,** on the site of the original jail, offers insights into crime and punishment and has a worn execution block on show.

Clink St., SE1 • *The Golden Hinde:* www.goldenhinde.com, 020 7403 0123, ££, closed Dec. 24–25 • The Clink Prison Museum: www.clink.co.uk, 020 7403 0900, ££, closed Dec. 25 • Tube: London Bridge

SOUTH BANK

Southwark Cathedral

8 This elegant, historic building served as a church for a medieval Augustinian monastery before becoming a cathedral in 1905, when it was refurbished. Its many interesting wood carvings include a 13th-century effigy of a recumbent knight and the **Great Screen** behind the altar, installed in 1520. The **Harvard Chapel** reminds visitors that John Harvard, founder of Harvard University, was baptized here in 1607. In the choir, the **Humble Monument** to merchant Richard Humble was carved circa 1616 by a group of Flemish refugee sculptors who belonged to the Southwark School of stonemasons. The church's theater connections date from Elizabethan times and are attested in the nave by a much later stained-glass window (1954) and statue (1912) to Shakespeare—whose spring birthday is celebrated here annually—and a memorial to American actor and director Sam Wanamaker, the driving force behind the rebuilding of the Globe in the 1990s. The cathedral is a popular concert venue, and the churchyard attracts picnickers from the adjacent **Borough Market** (see p. 82).

London Bridge, SE1 • http://cathedral.southwark.anglican.org • 020 7367 6700 • Donations requested • Tube: London Bridge

Butler's Wharf

9 A wander along Shad Thames on the east side of **Tower Bridge** brings you to Butler's Wharf and a canyon of renovated, 19th-century brick warehouses. Imagine cargo swinging from large cranes or rattling along the cobbled stones on iron-wheeled carts. Butler's Wharf housed the largest tea warehouse in the British Empire, and today tea and much else is for sale here in the specialist stores and restaurants. Enjoy al fresco dining on the promenade in the shadow of Tower Bridge.

Butler's Wharf, SE1 • Tube: London Bridge

High-level walkways across Shad Thames were once used for moving cargo between warehouses.

Tate Modern

*The latest works by contemporary artists join forces
with the nation's collection of 20th-century art.*

Tate Modern occupies the former Bankside power station on the bank of the Thames.

The move to a spacious new riverside location in 2000 allowed the Tate's
modern art collection to be displayed in a new way. Works from the landmark
art movements of the 20th century, including surrealism, abstract
expressionism, and pop art, are grouped thematically to show how they
overlapped with and influenced the work of other artists, and how later
artists, sometimes working in different media, responded to them. The gallery
also shows major loan exhibitions.

■ TURBINE HALL

Every year an artist of international renown is invited to create an installation in the vast Turbine Hall, greeting visitors as they enter the building. Previous artists have included Louise Bourgeois and Anish Kapoor, so expect the spectacular and thought-provoking.

■ SURREAL LANDSCAPES

On Level 3, surrealism is represented by the work of such great exponents as Salvador Dalí and René Magritte. Don't miss Dalí's **"Mountain Lake"** and George de Chirico's **"The Melancholy of Departure."** Nearby is Pablo Picasso's **"Head of a Woman,"** which was influenced by surrealism.

■ MONET'S INFLUENCE

Claude Monet's evocations of light and atmosphere in his later paintings influenced some of the abstract expressionists. His **"Water-Lilies,"** a semiabstract study of patterns of light on water, hangs next to the glowing yellow tones of Mark Rothko's **"Untitled circa 1950–52."** A Jackson Pollock drip painting, **"Summertime: Number 9A,"** is nearby.

■ ROTHKO ROOM

Also on Level 3, check out the group of paintings donated to the Tate by Mark Rothko. Shown in a small room with subdued light, their shimmering surfaces create a meditative mood.

■ FACE OF A MASTER

Among the expressionist masterpieces, look out for André Derain's **portrait of Henri Matisse,** worked with bold brushstrokes and non-naturalistic colors.

■ CUBISM

On Level 4, Pablo Picasso's **"Bust of a Woman"** and Georges Braque's **"Bottle and Fishes"** are fine examples from the pioneers of this early 20th-century movement. Cubist collages influenced the phenomenon of pop art, of which Roy Lichtenstein's **"Whaam!"** is a famous example.

SOUTH BANK

Bankside, SE1 • www.tate.org.uk/modern • 020 7887 8888 • Free except for major loan exhibitions • Closed Dec. 24–26 • Tube: Southwark or Mansion House

Shakespeare's City

London in the late 16th and early 17th centuries was a colorful, noisy, bustling place. From the monarch to the humblest apprentice, Londoners loved pageantry, music, and spectacle, not only on state occasions but also at the city authorities' brilliant street and river parades. It is no wonder that they embraced the new form of entertainment provided by the theaters and that William Shakespeare, the self-made man of native genius, shot to fame.

Shakespeare's memorial in Southwark Cathedral (above); theatergoers clutch red cushions (right) to pad the Globe's hard wooden seats.

A Captive Audience

When William Shakespeare arrived in London from Stratford-upon-Avon around 1588, he was, knowingly or not, making an astute career move. With a population approaching 200,000, flourishing London was England's biggest city.

Shakespeare Takes the Stage

The Bard emerged from obscurity in 1592, when he is mentioned for the first time as a player and dramatist on the London scene. He was a member of the Chamberlain's Men, a company of actors based at The Theatre in Shoreditch, London's first playhouse. Seven years later they moved south across the river to the new Globe.

The Globe became the largest Elizabethan theater, accommodating audiences 3,000 strong. Open to the elements, it was used only in summer; in winter the company retreated indoors to the Blackfriars Playhouse. Alerted by trumpet calls to the latest production, theatergoers would pay a few coins, collected in a box—hence the modern

SOUTH BANK

term "box office"—and stand at ground level or sit in tiered seats around the stage. Actors might be loudly encouraged or abused, and acrobats and jugglers provided entertainment between acts.

The pace of writing and production was frenetic, and the varied repertoire meant that Shakespeare ventured into lyrical comedies, dark tragedies, and Roman plays. His works for the Chamberlain's Men included the three parts of *Henry VI* and *Richard III*. The company performed regularly for Queen Elizabeth I and later—renamed the King's Men—for King James I. No plays were attributed to Shakespeare after 1613, and he died at Stratford in 1616.

THE MODERN **GLOBE THEATRE**

Shakespeare's Globe was demolished in 1644 by the Puritans during the English Civil War. Almost 350 years later, the American actor and film director Sam Wanamaker initiated the re-creation of the Globe. The open-air playhouse was built on a site close to the original. Inside are wooden galleries, a platform stage, and a circular pit where the audience stands to watch the play (see p. 76).

(see p. 76)

SOUTH BANK

Food Markets

With London's recent rise as a foodie capital, eating and shopping for food have come close to being competitive sports. Borough Market is London's premier food shopping experience, but artisanal foods and farmers markets can be found in other areas of the city.

■ BOROUGH MARKET

More than 130 stalls in this South Bank market sell a mix of artisanal, organic, and local produce. At each one, traders wax lyrical about their wares, which include chocolates, home-cured salamis, and raw-milk cheeses. Breathe in mouthwatering smells as you meander from stall to stall, stopping perhaps for grilled Swiss raclette (cheese) slathered over boiled potatoes and gherkins. Or choose a meringue from the top of a crispy tower at one of the many patisseries. Butchers at **The Ginger Pig** offer advice on how to cook their fine meats, and fruit and vegetable stalls are piled high with colorful varieties of tomatoes and much more. Rest your legs at **Maria's Market Cafe**—a market institution that serves up baps (soft rolls) filled with meaty delights.

Stoney St., SE1 • www.boroughmarket.org.uk • 020 7407 1002 • Closed Sun.–Wed. • Tube: London Bridge

■ AROUND BOROUGH

Across from the market, pop into **Neal's Yard Dairy** (6 Park St., SE1) to sample some of Britain's best farmhouse cheeses in a warehouse-like space whose walls are lined with clothbound cheddar. Next door is **Monmouth Coffee** (2 Park St., SE1), where carefully selected beans are ground to order and served with cakes and pastries. The smell of chorizo sandwiches wafts from the grill outside **Brindisa** (18–20 Southwark St., SE1), which has a peerless selection of Spanish cheeses and meats.

■ WHITECROSS STREET MARKET

One of the oldest markets in London, this Islington institution has been open for business since the 17th century. Specializing in local and regional produce, the market offers an array of culinary delights. As well as the usual fruit and vegetable stalls

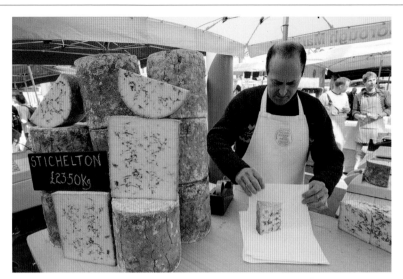

You can find expert cheesemakers from all over the United Kingdom at Borough Market.

throughout the week, on Thursday and Friday you will find specialist vendors of locally made cheeses, breads, cakes, pastries, pickles, and preserves. At lunchtime, the market offers an eclectic selection of street food from around the globe to hungry office workers.

Whitecross St., EC1 • www.whitecrossstreet .co.uk • 020 7527 1761 • Closed Sat. and Sun. • Tube: Old Street, Barbican, or Moorgate

■ PIMLICO ROAD FARMERS MARKET
It may be a relatively recent arrival, but Pimlico Road Farmers Market in Chelsea is fast gaining a reputation for

providing the very best in seasonal, organic fruits and vegetables, dairy products, meat, poultry, game, and preserves, all locally sourced from farms and producers. You can even buy a variety of freshly caught seafood from the East Anglian coast, including Essex oysters (in season). Hot food stalls are scarce, so you may wish to work up an appetite at the market and then eat lunch nearby on or around fashionable Sloane Square (see p. 148), a short stroll away along Bourne Street.

Intersection of Ebury St. and Pimlico Rd., SW1 • www.lfm.org.uk • 020 7833 0338 • Open Sat. a.m. • Tube: Sloane Square

Trafalgar Square & Soho

From the top of his lofty column, Admiral Lord Nelson looks down on the ebbing and flowing crowds in Trafalgar Square as people hurry to other destinations, rest by the fountains, or throng the entrance to the National Gallery on the square's north side. Across the road, the church of St. Martin-in-the-Fields provides an atmospheric setting for candlelight concerts. Leicester Square is the place to see the latest movies or find a theater seat at the half-price ticket booth. Wedged between Leicester Square and the theaters on Shaftesbury Avenue, Chinatown buzzes with Asian restaurants, while European immigrants have brought a continental flavor to Soho, where the sound of jazz spills out of the clubs. All of these destinations are within a stone's throw of each other.

◀ **Designed by architect Sir Charles Barry on a site that had been used to stable the monarch's horses, Trafalgar Square took shape in the 1840s.**

Trafalgar Square & Soho

Stroll through the West End, where theaters, cinemas, and restaurants abound, and feel the excitement of all that the city has to offer.

⑧ Chinatown (see p. 91) Revel in one of the liveliest, most colorful areas of the city, bustling with restaurants, food shops, and stalls, then cross back over Shaftesbury Avenue and stroll up Frith Street to Soho Square.

⑨ Soho Square (see p. 91) The square's gardens, near the lively restaurant area around Frith and Greek Streets, make a pleasant spot for a picnic and to enjoy open-air concerts in summer. Movie companies and advertising agencies surround the square.

⑦ Shaftesbury Avenue (see pp. 90–91) Stroll up this street of traditional theaters, where red velvet and golden cherubs encircle boxes rising majestically toward "the gods." Turn south onto Wardour Street and east onto Gerrard Street.

OXFORD STREET

ST. GILES HIGH ST.

Tottenham Court Road

CHARING CROSS ROAD

GREEK STREET

FRITH STREET

SOHO SQUARE ⑨

DEAN STREET

OLD COMPTON ST.

S O H O

WARDOUR STREET

BERWICK STREET

CARNABY STREET

0
0
300 meters
300 yards

5 Leicester Square (see pp. 89–90) Watch for movie stars' handprints paving the square where major motion pictures premiere. Leave from the northwest corner and stroll along Coventry Street to Piccadilly Circus.

4 St. Martin-in-the-Fields (see p. 89) Step inside this 18th-century church and stay perhaps for a concert or a bite to eat in the café. On leaving, head north on St. Martin's Place and turn left onto Irving Street.

1 Trafalgar Square (see p. 88) Begin where all London meets, by the fountains beneath Nelson's Column, then cross the square to the National Gallery on the north side.

2 National Gallery (see pp. 92–93) Check out one of the world's most impressive collections of Western European art. Outside, turn left and go around the side to St. Martin's Place.

3 National Portrait Gallery (see p. 88) From kings and queens to politicians and pop stars, this is where you can put faces to familiar names, then cross St. Martin's Place to St. Martin-in-the-Fields.

6 Piccadilly Circus (see p. 90) Pause to view the statue of Eros in Piccadilly Circus, the symbol of London's West End—a changing area of constant amusement— then turn up Shaftesbury Avenue.

TRAFALGAR SQUARE & SOHO DISTANCE: 2 MILES (3.2 KM)
TIME: APPROX. 6–8 HOURS TUBE START: CHARING CROSS

Trafalgar Square

1 Admiral Horatio Lord Nelson was cut down at the moment of victory in the naval battle off Cape Trafalgar in southwest Spain in 1805, while engaging the combined Spanish and French fleets of Napoleon Bonaparte. Glory lives on in the square, a place of enjoyment for all Londoners and a frequent focus for rallies and demonstrations, festivals, and concerts.

Nelson's Column, designed by William Railton, was erected in 1843. Four lions by the Victorian artist Sir Edwin Landseer guard the column, and friezes illustrating Nelson's sea victories, cast in bronze from captured cannon, decorate the base. The **Fourth Plinth,** in the square's northwest corner, features a changing exhibit of contemporary art.

Intersection of Charing Cross Rd. and the Strand • www.london .gov.uk/trafalgarsquare • Tube: Charing Cross or Embankment

IN **THE KNOW**

Nelson's Column stands 170 feet (52 m) high, including the hero's figure at 18 feet (5.5 m) tall. The top of the column on which the statue rests is so large it is said that, when it was erected, a dining table was placed on it and 14 stonemasons sat down to eat.

National Gallery

2 See pp. 92–93.

Trafalgar Sq., WC2 • www.nationalgallery.org.uk • 020 7747 2885 • Temporary exhibitions: £££ • Closed Jan. 1 and Dec. 24–26 • Tube: Charing Cross or Leicester Square

National Portrait Gallery

3 Studies of famous living people and heroes from British history, politics, sports, and the arts feature among the National Portrait Gallery's ever-expanding showcase. Seek out Marcus Gheeraerts's painting of the richly attired Queen Elizabeth I, highlight of the Tudor collection, and don't miss the only known contemporary portrait of playwright William Shakespeare. The ground floor shows an eclectic selection of 21st-century figures.

St. Martin's Pl., WC2 • www.npg.org.uk • 020 7306 0055 • Temporary exhibitions: £££ • Closed Dec. 24–26 • Tube: Charing Cross or Leicester Square

The National Gallery, left, and St. Martin-in-the-Fields, center, overlook Trafalgar Square.

St. Martin-in-the-Fields

4 If this royal church built by James Gibbs in 1726 looks familiar, it is because it has been much copied, especially in New England. The royal coat of arms above the colonnaded entrance indicates that it is the parish church for Buckingham Palace—you can see the royal box on the left as you enter the restrained interior. Known for its music, the church hosts regular concerts. The **Café in the Crypt** (see p. 90) pulsates to jazz on Wednesday nights.

Trafalgar Sq., WC2 • www.stmartin-in-the-fields.org. • 020 7766 1100 • Closed Mon.–Fri. 1–2 p.m. and Sun. a.m. except for services and concerts • Tube: Charing Cross

Leicester Square

5 The red carpets are rolled out here for movie premiers. The square has long been an entertainment hub—the **Empire** on the north side was once a Victorian music hall—and now boasts several movie theaters and the **MTV UK studios**. Movie stars' limousines aside, this is a pedestrianized area, and on the sidewalks you can stargaze for handprints of Clint Eastwood, Helena Bonham Carter, and others. Statues of William Shakespeare and Charlie Chaplain grace the gardens. The half-price ticket booth, **tkts** (*www.tkts.co.uk*), is the place for same-day theater seats.

Between Coventry St., W1, and Cranbourn St., WC2
• Tube: Leicester Square or Piccadilly Circus

Piccadilly Circus

6 A few steps west of Leicester Square, the figure of **Eros**, erected in Piccadilly in 1893, marks the heart of the West End's theaterland. Around this timeless statue, ever changing entertainment venues come and go. The sites of the former London Pavilion music hall and neighboring onetime Palace of Varieties have been transformed into the **Trocadero** shopping mall and entertainment center. Other venues are reassuringly constant: The **Criterion Theatre** (*2 Jermyn St., W1, 0844 847 1778*) remains sited below ground, and the fabulously decorated Criterion bar and restaurant (*224 Piccadilly, W1, 020 7930 0488, £££££*) is a visual treat. Piccadilly's neon Coca-Cola sign has beamed across the Circus since 1955.

Intersection of Piccadilly and Regent St., W1
• Tube: Piccadilly Circus

Shaftesbury Avenue

7 Philanthropist Anthony Lord Shaftesbury cleared slums in the 1880s to create Shaftesbury Avenue, running northeast from Piccadilly Circus. Many West End theaters have congregated here. All exude Edwardian grandeur—take a peek at their foyers. **The Lyric** (*No. 29*) is the oldest, built in 1888; the **Apollo**

GOOD **EATS**

■ **CAFÉ IN THE CRYPT**
A Londoners' favorite below St. Martin-in-the-Fields, serving hot and cold dishes. Bread-and-butter pudding with a topping of custard is a specialty.
Trafalgar Sq., WC2, 020 7766 1158, £

■ **PATISSERIE VALERIE**
Sample cake-making as an art form in this long-established café or snack on scrambled eggs and quiche.
44 Old Compton St., W1, 020 7437 3466, ££

■ **PORTRAIT BAR AND RESTAURANT**
Have breakfast, lunch, or tea at the top of the National Portrait Gallery while enjoying a bird's-eye view of Trafalgar Square.
St. Martin's Pl., WC2, 020 7312 2490, ££££

(No. 31) houses the steepest upper gallery in London. The two giants, both seating around 1,400 and dating from 1911, are the **Palace Theatre** *(No. 109)* and the **Shaftesbury** *(No. 210)*. Built as the Royal English Opera House, the Palace has long been popular for musicals—*Les Misérables* ran here for 18 years—while the Shaftesbury throbbed to the 1960s hit, *Hair*.

www.londontheatredirect.com • Tube: Piccadilly Circus, Leicester Square, or Tottenham Court Road

Chinatown

On Sundays, St. Martin-in-the-Fields (see p. 89) holds services in Cantonese and Mandarin for the local Chinese population. Red-and-gold gateways herald the way to a collection of pedestrian streets based around **Gerrard Street** on the south side of Shaftesbury Avenue. More than 70 restaurants, serving Cantonese, Szechuan, Japanese, Thai, and Malaysian foods, among others, provide ample choice. Have a specialty tea in Jen Café *(4–8 Newport Pl., WC2, ££)*, where you can see dumplings being rolled in the window. Always lively, Chinatown explodes with excitement during Chinese New Year (late January or early February).

Intersection of Shaftesbury Ave. and Whitcomb St., W1 • www.chinatownlondon.org • Tube: Leicester Square, Piccadilly Circus, or Tottenham Court Road

Soho Square

Workers and shoppers alike are drawn to the attractive garden in Soho Square, a summer venue for free concerts and festivals. The **statue of King Charles II** is a reminder that the square was once called King's Square and was one of the most fashionable addresses in town. Today it lies at the heart of the U.K.'s film industry.

Intersection of Greek St. and Sutton Row, W1 • Tube: Tottenham Court Road

More than 50 shops serving the needs of London's Chinese community cluster in and around Gerrard Street.

National Gallery

Founded in 1824, the national collection of Western European painting contains a rich and varied range of works by the great masters.

The National Gallery's collection comprises more than 2,300 works of art.

The National Gallery houses one of the world's great art collections, tracing the story of Western European painting from the early 13th century to the turn of the 20th. The collection is arranged chronologically, starting with the early Renaissance galleries in the Sainsbury Wing, continuing in the main building with the great masters of the 16th to 19th centuries, and ending with the Postimpressionists. Free admission to the permanent collection underpins the gallery's founding principle of "art for all."

■ FAVORITE SCENES

Start in the newest part of the gallery, the Sainsbury Wing, where the oldest paintings in the collection hang. During the early Renaissance (13th–15th centuries) most paintings had religious subjects, but portraits and scenes from history were also popular. Check out **"The Arnolfini Portrait"** (Room 56) by Van Eyck, an early master of oil painting, and Piero's **"Baptism of Christ"** (Room 66), set in a Tuscan landscape.

■ CARTOONS & MYSTERIES

Walk through to the main building's West Wing, where the story of the Renaissance continues. Among the star exhibits are Leonardo da Vinci's cartoon (drawing) of the **"Virgin and Child"** (Room 51). If you enjoy mysteries, look at Hans Holbein's **"The Ambassadors"** (Room C). This portrait of two young men also contains a distorted skull, provoking much debate about its meaning.

■ COURT TO COUNTRY

The rooms in the North Wing introduce Dutch and French artists from the 17th century. A highlight

among London court painter Anthony van Dyck's works is **"Equestrian Portrait of Charles I"** (Room 31).

For 19th-century British painting don't miss Room 34 in the East Wing. Masterpieces on show include John Constable's landscape **"The Hay Wain"** and J. M. W. Turner's ethereal **"Rain, Steam, and Speed."**

■ IMPRESSIONISM & POSTIMPRESSIONISM

Among the Impressionists, Claude Monet is well represented—seek out **"Bathers at La Grenouillère"** (Room 43) from 1869. Postimpressionist Paul Cézanne's **"Bathers"** hangs in Room 45. In the same room you can see **"Chair," "Sunflowers,"** and **"A Wheatfield, with Cypresses,"** all by Vincent van Gogh.

Trafalgar Sq., WC2 • www.nationalgallery.org.uk • 020 7747 2885 • Loan exhibitions: £££ • Closed Jan. 1 and Dec. 24–26 • Tube: Charing Cross, Leicester Square, or Embankment

Pub Culture

Inns, taverns, and alehouses—the forerunners of today's pubs—have been part of the London scene for hundreds of years. You can spot a pub—short for "public house"—by its artistic signage and often quaint exterior. Here, as long ago, travelers find refreshment, workers take time out, and friends relax together. Order a "pint of bitter," the traditional tipple, from the bar or choose from a multitude of other beverages.

TRAFALGAR SQUARE & SOHO

Many old pubs, like Ye Olde Cheshire Cheese (above), have small, cozy bars; a refreshing pint of chilled lager (right).

Monks & Medieval Inns

The pub has its roots in the inns, taverns, and alehouses of medieval London. Of these, the Tabard Inn in Southwark was immortalized in literature. There, the 14th-century poet Geoffrey Chaucer's pilgrims gathered at the start of *The Canterbury Tales.* As with many such places, it had monastic associations. Its founder was an abbot, who wanted a base when he or his monks came up to the capital. You can still refresh yourself at its close neighbor, **The George** *(77 Borough High St., SE1, 020 7407 2056),* a galleried coaching inn.

Home Brew

In medieval times, inns such as the Tabard and George provided food, drink, and beds for wealthy wayfarers. Taverns offered food washed down with wine, while alehouses served ale and simple fare for poorer people. Many alehouses were run by women, who made ale for their families, as it was safer to drink than city water. In 1500, the introduction of the tangy-flavored hop from Germany, which produced a longer-lasting beer, heralded the arrival of specialized breweries, and alehouses became more sophisticated.

Glitzy Decor

In the 17th century, Londoners developed a taste for cheap gin, which by the 19th century was being served in "gin palaces." These premises offered unheard-of luxuries to working-class Londoners—plate-glass windows, mirrors, and gas lighting. Pubs (as alehouses and inns were becoming known) followed suit with luxurious new premises, such as the **Princess Louise** *(208 High Holborn, WC1, 020 7405 8816)*, built in 1872. The late 19th century brought a boom in pub building; no new suburb was complete without its parish church and its pub.

ALL IN **A NAME**

Pub names often tell a story. Several are called The Marquis of Granby after a general in the 1700s who paid to set up wounded soldiers as pub-keepers. Crossed Keys are named for St. Peter, who was said to hold the keys to heaven. Red Lions, heraldic symbol of Scotland, hark back to the coronation of King James VI of Scotland as James I of England. And Bears would have held bear-baiting events.

Gourmet Eating

There is no shortage of fine-dining opportunities in London, a city replete with 53 Michelin-starred restaurants. Visiting foodies can sample outstanding cuisine, artfully crafted by top-name chefs and their award-winning protégés. Modern British, gourmet French, light Italian—the choice is yours.

■ SOHO

Once called London's larder, Soho was the birthplace of the city's gourmet restaurant scene, and it is still home to some of the original restaurants. **Quo Vadis** (*26–29 Dean St., W1, 020 437 9585, ££–££££*), which opened in 1926, excels at modern British cuisine served in its elegant rooms. For celebrity-spotting try **The Ivy** (*1–5 West St., WC2, 020 7836 4751, £££–£££££*), established in Covent Garden in 1917, which serves an updated version of an Edwardian chophouse menu. **Bob Bob Ricard** (*1 Upper James St., W1, 020 3145 1000, £££–££££*) is one of the starriest settings for dining, with brass "press for Champagne" buttons at each table.

■ A SOURCE OF INSPIRATION

One of London's most influential restaurants was opened in Mayfair in 1967 by the Roux family. **Le Gavroche** (*43 Upper Brook St., W1, 020 7408 0881, £££££*) was the U.K.'s first restaurant to be awarded three Michelin stars (although later reduced to two). Chefs such as Marco Pierre White and Gordon Ramsay worked here before going on to have glittering careers of their own. In the 1980s, Fulham's **River Café** (*Thames Wharf, Rainville Rd., W6, 020 7386 4200, £££££*) and Chelsea's **Bibendum** (*Michelin House, 81 Fulham Rd., SW3, 020 7581 5817, £££££*) introduced light, modern takes on Italian and French cuisine, respectively, and are still popular with diners.

■ HIGH-END HOTEL DINING

Recent years have seen a boom in gourmet dining at London's upscale hotels. Top of anyone's list, with a three-month waiting list, is Heston Blumenthal's **Dinner** (*66 Knightsbridge, SW1, 020 7201 3833,*

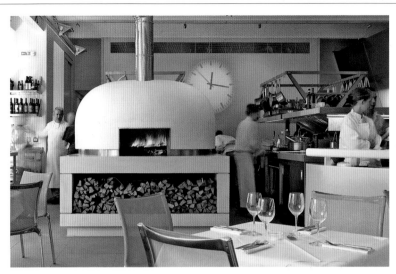

The Italian menu changes twice daily at the River Café, on the banks of the Thames at Fulham.

££££££) at the Mandarin Oriental, near Harrods. The celebrity chef's unique approach to cooking includes fresh interpretations of historic dishes, such as Powdered Duck (the dish originated in around 1670). For fabulous French fare, head to Mayfair and **Hélène Darroze at the Connaught** (*Carlos Pl., W1, 020 7107 8880, £££££*) or **Ducasse** (*Park Lane, W1, 020 7629 8866, £££££*) at the Dorchester, or to Knightsbridge and **Koffmann's** (*Wilton Pl., SW1, 020 7235 1010, £££–£££££*) at the Berkeley, which all offer seasonal dishes from across the English Channel. **Gordon Ramsay at Claridge's** (*Brook St., W1, 020 7499 0099, £££££*) in Mayfair serves a more broadly European menu.

■ THE NEXT GENERATION

For a less formal outing, watch for places run by young chefs who have trained at the city's great restaurants. Anna Hansen runs **The Modern Pantry** (*48 St. John's Sq., EC1, 020 7553 9210, ££££*) in Clerkenwell, offering a fresh approach on an East-meets-West theme. Anthony Demetre's **Arbutus** (*63–64 Frith St., W1, 020 7734 4545, ££–£££*) in Soho has won a string of awards for its modern European dishes.

Covent Garden to Ludgate Hill

The north bank of the Thames between Trafalgar Square and St. Paul's Cathedral on Ludgate Hill holds a warren of streets and alleys with a varied history. Given the raucous street performers and the mass of humanity that swirls through on a daily basis, it is hard to imagine that much of this area was once a tranquil "convent" garden tended by the monks of Westminster Abbey. Confiscated by the Crown during King Henry VIII's dissolution of the monasteries in the 1530s, Covent Garden later became a posh residential quarter. By Victorian times it was a thriving market, while the surrounding area included the hub of London's theater world, hangouts for writers, and the heart of Britain's legal system. Nowadays, the area is also notable for good eating and entertainment.

◀ **The market in Covent Garden provides a mix of shopping, relaxation, and refreshment.**

Covent Garden to Ludgate Hill

Opera and street performance rub shoulders with the British legal system in this area of broad streets and narrow alleys.

❶ Covent Garden (see p. 102) Good eats and great entertainment are the hallmarks of this former fruit, vegetable, and flower market. Walk to the west side of the Piazza.

❷ St. Paul's Covent Garden (see p. 102) The "Actor's Church" hosts religious services and a wide array of live entertainment, and has a great garden out back. Exit the Piazza's north side (James Street), turn right onto Floral Street, and then walk one block.

❸ Royal Opera House (see pp. 102–103) Home to Britain's premier opera and ballet companies, the theater boasts 300 years of performance history. Walk two blocks down Bow Street and right onto Tavistock Street.

❹ London Transport Museum (see p. 103) Learn about the world's first subway system, how the city kept moving during the Blitz, and other fascinating facts about London's transportation history. Walk two blocks down Burleigh Street and left onto the Strand.

**COVENT GARDEN TO LUDGATE HILL   DISTANCE: 2 MILES (3.2 KM)
TIME: APPROX. 6–8 HOURS   TUBE START: COVENT GARDEN**

9 St. Bride's Church (see p. 105) Fleet Street's patron church features Wren's "wedding cake" steeple and a crypt displaying archaeological remains from 2,000 years of history.

City (Thameslink)

8 Sir John Soane's Museum (see pp. 104–105) Rather like a miniature version of the British Museum, this was once the home of eccentric architect John Soane and his marvelous collections. Retrace your steps to the front of the Royal Courts. Turn left onto Fleet Street.

7 Royal Courts of Justice (see p. 104) London's legal eagles flock to a Gothic maze that is every bit as complicated as the laws that are enforced within. Follow Bell Yard, then Carey and Serle Streets to Lincoln's Inn Fields behind the R.C.J.

6 Courtauld Gallery & Somerset House (see pp. 106–107) Works by Van Gogh, Goya, Gainsborough, and many other artists grace the galleries at this world-class bastion of art history. Continue east on the Strand past St. Clement Danes.

5 The Strand (see pp. 103–104) This former Roman road along the northern shore of the Thames was later the haunt of actors, writers, and aristocrats. Keep heading east on the Strand.

Covent Garden

1 Master architect Inigo Jones designed the elegant **Piazza** and its colonnaded buildings in the 1630s as an aristocratic enclave. The square also attracted vendors hawking wares to the rich—a tiny seed of commerce that eventually bloomed into London's primary vegetable, fruit, and flower market. The market pavilion is late Georgian (1830), but for the most part Jones would still recognize the lovely square that he laid out nearly 400 years ago. Covent Garden's evolution into an energetic dining and entertainment hub began in the 1970s, when the food and flower markets moved south of the Thames. Although it looks chaotic at first glance, the **street theater** is carefully orchestrated: Musicians, acrobats, and other buskers must audition for a license to perform in the Piazza, and many have been playing Covent Garden for years.

Covent Garden Piazza, WC2 • www.coventgardenlondonuk.com • Tube: Covent Garden, Leicester Square, or Charing Cross

St. Paul's Covent Garden

2 Called the "Actor's Church" because of its affiliation with the local theater world, St. Paul's is another Inigo Jones creation. The facade and its husky Tuscan columns feature in the first scene of George Bernard Shaw's *Pygmalion,* the play that introduced Covent Garden flowergirl Eliza Doolittle. Inside, look out for the plaques commemorating **Vivien Leigh, Charlie Chaplin,** and **Boris Karloff.** Little known to the milling hordes out front, the church's **back garden** is a peaceful oasis amid the hubbub of central London.

Bedford St., WC2 • www.actorschurch.org • 020 7836 5221• Tube: Covent Garden

Royal Opera House

3 From the composer George Frideric Handel and the actor Edmund Kean to the opera singer Jenny Lind and the ballerina Margot Fonteyn, countless great names of stage, music, and dance have played this legendary theater on the northeastern edge of

Covent Garden. The present building (opened in 1858) is the third on the site; fire destroyed the first two. The elegant Corinthian portico fronts a massive auditorium that can seat more than 2,200 patrons for performances by the Royal Opera and Royal Ballet. A program of exhibitions celebrates past productions and visiting companies.

Bow St., WC2 • www.roh.org.uk • 020 7304 4000 • Tours £££
• Tube: Covent Garden

London Transport Museum

4 This museum on the southeast side of Covent Garden tracks 200 years of London's urban transport. Its vast interior (once a flower market) brims, like a Matchbox collection gone mad, with old taxis, trams, Tube cars, carriages, and double-decker buses. Highlights include an old horse-drawn bus, an 1866 steam engine, and an early motor bus. Vintage posters and uniforms complement the vehicles.

Covent Garden Piazza, WC2 • www.ltmuseum.co.uk • 020 7379 6344 • ££££
• Tube: Covent Garden

Visitors to the Royal Opera House sip Champagne in the ornate iron-and-glass Paul Hamlyn Hall, formerly part of the flower market.

The Strand

5 Running 0.75 of a mile (1 km) between Trafalgar Square and Fleet Street, the Strand is one of London's most storied thoroughfares. As the name implies, this was once the north bank of the Thames. It has been a roadway since Roman times, and during the Middle Ages it was lined with palaces. By the Victorian era, it had morphed into a theater hub and literary hangout for the likes of Charles Dickens. Flanked by the **Royal Courts of Justice** (see p. 104) and, at its eastern end, the **Inns of Court** (see pp. 108–109), the street remains the nucleus of London's legal world, while the posh **Savoy Hotel** (1889) is a reminder that Britain's luxury-hotel heritage also began on the Strand. "Islands" in the street host the churches of **St. Mary le Strand** (1717) and **St. Clement Danes** (1681).

Between Trafalgar Sq. and Fleet St. • Tube: Charing Cross or Embankment

Courtauld Gallery & Somerset House

6 See pp. 106–107.

Somerset House, Strand, WC2 • www.courtauld.ac.uk • 020 7872 0220 • ££ • Closed Dec. 25–26 • Tube: Temple, Embankment, or Charing Cross

Royal Courts of Justice

7 Clinging to legal traditions that stretch back nearly a thousand years, white-wigged judges and lawyers scurry through the maze of hallways, passages, and rooms that compose the geographic heart of British justice. This neo-Gothic labyrinth was constructed in the late 19th century, and its 88 courtrooms hear many of the nation's most serious civil cases. The imposing main entrance—more like that of a cathedral than a civic building—leads into a **Great Hall** that measures 80 feet (24 m) in height and 238 feet (72 m) in length. The public is free to attend most cases.

Strand, WC2 • www.justice.gov.uk • 020 7947 7684 • Advance reservation required for tours • Tube: Temple or Charing Cross

Sir John Soane's Museum

8 A man for all seasons, Georgian-era architect John Soane had a keen eye for collecting and bequeathed this sprawling house with its eclectic contents to the British nation. The collection runs a broad gamut from Egyptian and Roman antiquities to paintings by **Hogarth, Canaletto,** and **Turner,** as well as stained glass, rare books,

COVENT GARDEN TO LUDGATE HILL

GOOD **EATS**

■ **AXIS**
Stylish modern decor and cutting-edge cuisine make this restaurant inside the One Aldwych hotel one of London's premier taste treats. **1 Aldwych, WC2, 020 7300 1000, ££££**

■ **CHEZ GÉRARD**
The quintessential Covent Garden café serves up French classics (escargot, steak frites, confit de canard) and al fresco eating overlooking the Piazza. **The Piazza, WC2, 0207 379 0666, £££**

■ **LOCH FYNE**
Inspired by the seafood of the Scottish coast, the menu includes oysters, mussels, and smoked salmon. The restaurant is on a quiet street just east of the Piazza. **2–4 Catherine St., WC2, 020 7240 4999, £££**

In Sir John Soane's picture room, paintings hang on panels that open to reveal more paintings.

timepieces, furniture, Chinese tiles, and odds and ends salvaged from other buildings. Contents aside, the house offers a rare, almost undisturbed glimpse of cultured, upper middle-class London life in the early 19th century.

13 Lincoln's Inn Fields, WC2 • www.soane.org • 020 7405 2107 • Tours ££
• Closed Sun. and Mon. • Tube: Holborn or Chancery Lane

St. Bride's Church

9 World War II bombing almost destroyed the patron church of London's newspaper business, but the church was rebuilt to Sir Christopher Wren's original design. A 226-foot (69 m) tiered **"wedding-cake" steeple**—the only part that survived the Blitz—crowns the church. The crypt houses a museum, a collection of historic gravestones, and a rare **iron coffin** designed to thwart grave robbers.

Fleet St., EC4 • www.stbrides.com • 020 7427 0133 • Tube: Temple, Blackfriars, or St. Paul's

Courtauld Gallery & Somerset House

One of the world's most famous small art collections

The gallery's intimate rooms house Impressionist and Postimpressionist masterpieces.

The Courtauld Gallery is situated in one of the most beautiful 18th-century buildings in London, William Chambers' Somerset House, overlooking the Thames. Textiles millionaire Samuel Courtauld and other private collectors established the gallery's collection, which embraces European painting, sculpture, and decorative arts from the medieval to the modern periods, in the 19th and 20th centuries. The collection is most famous for its paintings by Monet, Renoir, Manet, Cézanne, Gauguin, and van Gogh.

COVENT GARDEN TO LUDGATE HILL

■ MEDIEVAL ART

The first room displays medieval and early Italian Renaissance paintings. It also includes the sumptuous early Netherlandish triptych **"Entombment of Christ"** by the Master of Flemalle and exquisite **Gothic ivories** (1270–1400), which were used for personal meditation.

■ THE RENAISSANCE

The splendor of art in 15th- and 16th-century Italy is represented by the spectacular pair of gold and painted marriage chests (called *cassoni*). Botticelli's **"The Trinity"** was originally painted for the high altar of the Florentine convent of repentant prostitutes (*convertite*) and preaches Christian virtue. The northern Renaissance is represented by painter Lucas Cranach's exquisitely detailed **"Adam and Eve,"** a harmonious image of Paradise before the fall, with a naturalistic depiction of lions, sheep, and naked bodies.

■ RUBENS & BAROQUE

Versatile baroque master Peter Paul Rubens is especially well represented with landscapes, oil sketches, a design

for his famous altarpiece the **"Descent from the Cross,"** and the touching family portrait **"Family of Jan Brueghel,"** depicting friends of the artist. Works by Anthony van Dyck, Goya, and Tiepolo are nearby.

■ IMPRESSIONIST & POSTIMPRESSIONIST

The highlights of the gallery's collection are the modern masterpieces, including Edouard Manet's **"A Bar at the Folies-Bergère,"** Pierre-Auguste Renoir's **"La Loge,"** Vincent van Gogh's **"Self-Portrait with Bandaged Ear,"** and works by Claude Monet, Edgar Degas, and Paul Gauguin.

A whole room is devoted to Britain's finest collection of paintings by Paul Cézanne, including his iconic Provençal landscape, **"Montaigne Ste.-Victoire."**

Somerset House, Strand, WC2 • www.courtauld.ac.uk • 020 7872 0220 • ££ • Closed Dec. 25–26 • Tube: Temple, Embankment, or Charing Cross

Legal Traditions

Like the monarchy, the British legal system has succeeded in adapting to the modern world while retaining picturesque and archaic customs, dress, and procedures. In central London, the Inns of Court—where many lawyers have their offices—and the Courts themselves are treasuries of history as well as working parts of the contemporary legal system. Their gardens provide some of London's most tranquil green spaces.

COVENT GARDEN TO LUDGATE HILL

The Royal Courts of Justice clock (above); lawyers wearing their ceremonial wigs and robes process into a church service (right).

Inns of Court

All barristers (lawyers who act as advocates in court) in England and Wales must be members of one of four associations known collectively as the Inns of Court. These communities of lawyers established themselves on land between the City of London and Westminster around 700 years ago. Two of the Inns of Court, the Inner Temple and Middle Temple, lie between the Thames and Fleet Street. An easy stroll north from Fleet Street along Chancery Lane leads toward the other two, Lincoln's Inn and Gray's Inn.

Providing everything a group of learned men needed—rooms to live and work in, a hall for dining, a church for prayer, a library for reading, and gardens for rest and relaxation—the Inns of Court are oases of cloistered calm in the city. Their walls enclose courtyards and narrow lanes as well as broad expanses of lawn and flowers. Wandering through the grounds of the Inns, visitors glimpse wigged and gowned lawyers heading from their offices to court, burdened with armfuls of files.

The Inner and Middle Temple are particularly rich in history. The 12th-century **Temple Church** (*Inner Temple Lane, WC2, www.templechurch.com, 020 7353 3470*) has a round nave modeled on the Church of the Holy Sepulchre in Jerusalem. Opposite stands the Tudor **Middle Temple Hall,** where the first performance of Shakespeare's comedy, *Twelfth Night,* took place on Candlemas, February 2, 1602.

The Courts

To see the law in action, just walk a short distance from the Inns of Court to the Royal Courts of Justice on the Strand (see p. 103) to hear civil cases, or to the Central Criminal Court at the **Old Bailey** (*Old Bailey, EC4, 020 7248 3277, closed weekends and public holidays*) for criminal cases.

FORMER MEMBERS OF THE **INNS OF COURT**

William Penn, founder of Pennsylvania, was a member of Lincoln's Inn.

Five signers of the American Declaration of Independence— Edward Rutledge, Thomas Heyward, Thomas McKean, Thomas Lynch, and Arthur Middleton—were members of the Middle Temple. Another signer, William Paca, was a member of the Inner Temple.

The young Charles Dickens was employed as a clerk in Gray's Inn.

House Museums

Writers, artists, statesmen, scientists—many of the great and good have made their homes in London. Whether filled with priceless art collections or the quotidian objects of daily existence, these houses provide glimpses into the lives and passions of their famous former occupants.

■ DR. JOHNSON'S HOUSE

Situated in a network of passages north of Fleet Street, 17 Gough Square was built around 1700. Dr. Samuel Johnson lived in the house from 1748 to 1759 and compiled his English dictionary here.

17 Gough Sq., EC4 • www.drjohnsonshouse .org • 020 7353 3745 • ££ • Closed Sun. and public holidays

■ JOHN WESLEY'S HOUSE

Founder of Methodism with his brother Charles, John Wesley built this house and adjacent chapel on the City's north edge in 1779. His belongings are preserved, as are his study and prayer room.

49 City Rd., EC1 • www.wesleyschapel.org.uk • 020 7253 2262 • Donations • Closed Sun. and public holidays

■ APSLEY HOUSE

Also known as Number One, London, Apsley House on Hyde Park Corner, Westminster, was designed by Robert Adam between 1771 and 1778. The first Duke of Wellington moved here after his victory over Napoleon at Waterloo in 1815. The art collection includes paintings by Velázquez and Rubens and a nude statue of Napoleon.

149 Piccadilly, W1 • www.english-heritage.org.uk • 020 7499 5676 • ££ • Closed Mon. (except public holidays), Tues., Jan. 1, Dec 24–26

■ BENJAMIN FRANKLIN HOUSE

This Georgian house off Trafalgar Square is the only surviving home of scientist, philosopher, and American founding father Dr. Benjamin Franklin, who lived here between 1757 and 1775.

36 Craven St., WC2 • www.benjaminfranklin house.org • 020 7839 2006 • ££ • Closed Mon.– Tues. • Reservation recommended

■ FREUD MUSEUM

Having escaped Austria after its annexation by Nazi Germany, Sigmund

In Dennis Severs' House, burning candles suggest that the original occupants are nearby.

Freud moved with his family to Hampstead. Here, you can see the couch used by his patients, his study, and his collection of nearly 2,000 Roman, Greek, Egyptian, and Oriental antiquities.

20 Maresfield Gdns., NW3 • www.freud.org.uk • 020 7435 2002 • ££ • Closed Mon.–Tues.

■ Linley Sambourne House

This late Victorian town house in Kensington was the home of *Punch* magazine cartoonist and illustrator Edward Linley Sambourne (1844–1910). The house retains much of the original furniture and other possessions of the Sambourne family, including a notable collection of Chinese export porcelain and English tin-glazed wares.

18 Stafford Ter., W8 • www.rbkc.gov.uk/subsites/ museums/18staffordterrace.aspx • 020 7602 3316 • ££ • Tours Wed. 11:15 a.m. and 2:15 p.m., Sat. and Sun. 11:15 a.m.

■ Dennis Severs' House

Would-be time travelers will delight in this Georgian house on Folgate Street in Spitalfields, East London. Visitors are led in silence through the ten rooms, each decorated in a different historical style.

18 Folgate St., E1 • www.dennissevershouse .co.uk • 020 7247 4013 • £££ • Open Sun. and every other Mon. • Twilight tour: Mon. p.m., reservation required

BLOOMSBURY

Bloomsbury

This is the city's intellectual heart, where several colleges of the University of London surround elegant garden squares. Here, in an area loosely bounded by Euston Road to the north and Holborn to the south, are some of the world's foremost repositories of knowledge, including the greatest museum and library in Britain. The architecture is commensurate with this cerebral atmosphere. Stately Georgian town houses mingle with classical churches, imposing art deco office buildings, and a striking neo-Gothic railroad station. In the early 20th century, the Bloomsbury literary set blossomed and revolutionaries espoused new ideologies in this bookish atmosphere. Diplomats have also made their homes here, as many embassies are based in the area. Bloomsbury is not just for the learned elite, however. Peaceful streets offer an oasis of calm. People of all ages will enjoy the old-fashioned playthings at Pollock's Toy Museum, and you don't have to be young to appreciate the Cartoon Museum's mischievous drawings.

◀ **The more than seven million artifacts in the British Museum's collection include a colossal bust of the Egyptian pharaoh Amenhotep III.**

Bloomsbury

Leafy squares, rows of brick and stone town houses,
and fabulous museums draw visitors to the area.

7 British Library
(see p. 119) **Every book
you could ever want can
be found here.** Head
east on Euston Road to
St. Pancras Station.

5 Pollock's Toy Museum
(see p. 118) **Visit this collection
of toys,** then return to
Tottenham Court Road and head
north. Turn east on Torrington
Place to Tavistock Place, and then
turn south on Hunter Street.

BLOOMSBURY DISTANCE: 2.6 MILES (4 KM)
TIME: APPROX. 8 HOURS TUBE START: HOLBORN

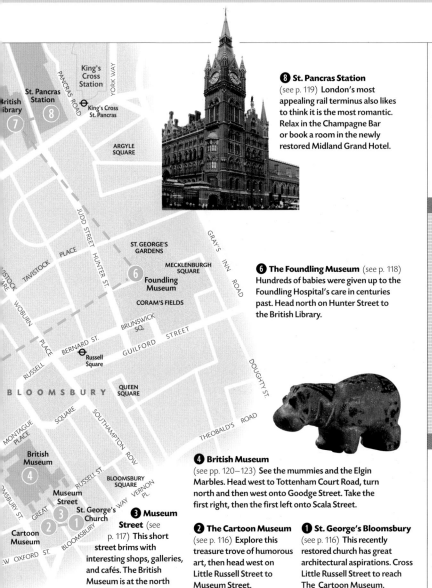

8 St. Pancras Station
(see p. 119) London's most appealing rail terminus also likes to think it is the most romantic. Relax in the Champagne Bar or book a room in the newly restored Midland Grand Hotel.

6 The Foundling Museum (see p. 118) Hundreds of babies were given up to the Foundling Hospital's care in centuries past. Head north on Hunter Street to the British Library.

4 British Museum
(see pp. 120–123) See the mummies and the Elgin Marbles. Head west to Tottenham Court Road, turn north and then west onto Goodge Street. Take the first right, then the first left onto Scala Street.

2 The Cartoon Museum (see p. 116) Explore this treasure trove of humorous art, then head west on Little Russell Street to Museum Street.

1 St. George's Bloomsbury (see p. 116) This recently restored church has great architectural aspirations. Cross Little Russell Street to reach The Cartoon Museum.

3 Museum Street (see p. 117) This short street brims with interesting shops, galleries, and cafés. The British Museum is at the north end of Museum Street.

Map labels:
King's Cross Station
St. Pancras Station
British Library
York Way
PANCRAS ROAD
King's Cross St. Pancras
ARGYLE SQUARE
JUDD STREET
TAVISTOCK PLACE
HUNTER ST.
ST. GEORGE'S GARDENS
MECKLENBURGH SQUARE
GRAY'S INN ROAD
6 Foundling Museum
CORAM'S FIELDS
WOBURN PLACE
RUSSELL SQUARE
BERNARD ST.
BRUNSWICK SQ.
GUILFORD STREET
Russell Square
DOUGHTY ST.
BLOOMSBURY
QUEEN SQUARE
MONTAGUE PLACE
SOUTHAMPTON ROW
THEOBALD'S ROAD
British Museum 4
RUSSELL ST.
BLOOMSBURY SQUARE
Museum Street
GREAT
BLOOMSBURY WAY
VERNON PL.
St. George's Church
Cartoon Museum
2 3 1
NEW OXFORD ST.

BLOOMSBURY

St. George's Bloomsbury

1 The final church designed by Sir Christopher Wren's protégé, Nicholas Hawksmoor, was consecrated in 1731 for Bloomsbury's newly established gentry. The church has a portico with Corinthian columns, based on the Roman temple of Bacchus in Baalbec, and the pyramid-like structure on its spire is influenced by Turkey's grand tomb of Mausoleus. The majestically simple interior has been recently restored and is regarded as a high-water mark in the English Baroque style. Its acoustics make it a popular concert venue, and the undercroft holds a permanent exhibition of the church's, and Bloomsbury's, history.

Little Russell St., WC1 • www.stgeorgesbloomsbury.org.uk • 020 7242 1979 • Tube: Holborn

GOOD **EATS**

■ **THE LAMB**
Traditional pub-grub and British beer are served in this historic Victorian bar, which has old-style frosted-glass screens for the privacy of the patrons.
94 Lambs Conduit St., WC1, 020 7405 0713, £

■ **MARY WARD CENTRE**
This adult education college's vegetarian café and art gallery is a hidden gem. Enjoy great value tasty food in a peaceful Georgian building.
42 Queen Sq., WC1, 020 7269 6000, £

■ **PIED À TERRE**
Delicious dishes from seasonal ingredients in a refined atmosphere have earned this restaurant two Michelin stars.
34 Charlotte St., W1, 020 7636 1178, £££££

The Cartoon Museum

2 London's only museum of humorous drawings contains hundreds of items, ranging from cutting political cartoons to original art from old and new children's comic books. The exhibits focus on British artists, beginning in the 18th century, when artists first used playful drawings to make serious political points, and follow the evolution of the cartoon from then through to 20th-century British children's comic classics, such as *The Beano* and *Dandy.* Some of the more recent political caricatures still cut to the bone, and World War I cartoons have retained their poignancy. The museum library contains more than 4,000 books on animation, comics, caricature, and cartoons.

35 Little Russell St., WC1 • www.cartoonmuseum.org • 020 7580 8155 • ££ • Closed Mon., Jan. 1, and Dec. 25–31 • Tube: Holborn

BLOOMSBURY

Just west of Museum Street, James Smith & Sons specializes in umbrellas.

Museum Street

3 Opposite the British Museum is Museum Street—a unique stretch of shops. On the corner is the **Museum Tavern,** whose Victorian interior of mahogany and etched glass is complemented by a range of good British beers. **Abbott and Holder** *(No. 30)* specializes in English paintings, drawings, and prints from the past 250 years. **Atlantis** *(No. 49a)* has been selling occult books since 1922. There are also shops selling reproductions of classical ceramics, statues, and many other interesting items.

Runs from New Oxford St. to Great Russell St. • Tube: Holborn

British Museum

4 See pp. 120–123.

Great Russell St., WC1 • www.britishmuseum.org • 020 7323 8299 • Closed Jan. 1 and Dec. 24–26 • Tube: Tottenham Court Road, Holborn, or Russell Square

BLOOMSBURY

Pollock's Toy Museum

5 A clutter of nostalgia—including a **World War I teddy bear** and a **19th-century rocking horse**—fill the rooms of two 18th- and 19th-century houses joined together to form this museum. The collection is based on the work of shopkeeper Benjamin Pollock, who produced toy theaters that could be assembled from sheets of printed card ("a penny plain, tuppence colored"). Pollock's original shop was in Hoxton, East London, and he kept it going from around 1880 until his death in 1937, by which time he was famous for his toys, with such clients as author Robert Louis Stevenson and art critic Serge Diaghilev.

1 Scala St., W1 • www.pollockstoymuseum.com • 020 7636 3452 • ££ • Closed Sun. and all public holidays • Tube: Goodge Street

The Foundling Museum

6 Seventy-five percent of children died before the age of five in mid-18th-century London, with 90 percent of them dying in the workhouse. The philanthropist Capt. Thomas Coram, appalled by such conditions, created the Foundling Hospital in 1739 to take care of the many unwanted babies. They arrived at a rate of around 200 a year, and their mothers often left them with keepsake bows, ribbons, bonnets, and sleeves embroidered with hearts or flowers. A heartrending collection of these mementos is on view. The museum is spread over three floors, displaying period interiors, exhibits of the hospital's history, and an extensive collection of memorabilia of composer George Frideric Handel, who was a benefactor. The large art collection includes paintings by William Hogarth, who also donated money to the hospital. The **Governors' Meeting Room** is described as having London's finest 18th-century rococo interior.

IN **THE KNOW**

Workhouses provided free food and lodging for the poor and unemployed in return for work. They also housed orphaned and abandoned kids.

40 Brunswick Sq., WC1 • www.foundlingmuseum.org.uk • 020 7841 3600 • £££ • Closed Mon. and public holidays • Tube: Russell Square

British Library

7 A copy of every book published in the United Kingdom and the Republic of Ireland is lodged with the British Library, requiring an estimated 6.8 miles (11 km) of new shelf space each year. The building surrounds the **King's Library,** a central glass-walled tower that holds a collection of large leather-bound books amassed by King George III. Although the reading rooms are only for researchers, visitors can enjoy the displays of treasures from the Library's archives, including some of the earliest printed **Shakespeare plays,** original **Beatles lyrics,** and the **Magna Carta.**

96 Euston Rd., NW1 • www.bl.uk • 0843 208 1144 • Closed Sun. and Dec. 25
• Tube: King's Cross St. Pancras

St. Pancras Station

8 This architectural gem, completed in 1868, is a neo-Gothic palace from the age of steam that is now the starting point for the high-speed Eurostar link to the Continent and the Javelin service to Stratford Olympic Park. Train travel has always been romantic, and in its refurbished form—columns repainted in their original blue, giving a feeling of open skies—St. Pancras sells itself as a place for courtship. The Champagne Bar, which claims to be Europe's longest, is one possibility. A statue of a kissing couple, titled **"Brief Encounter,"** looms over the concourse. More endearing is the statue of English poet **John Betjeman,** who was a champion of Victorian architecture. Old-world charm is provided at the **St. Pancras Renaissance Hotel** (see p. 184), which opened in the former Midland Grand Hotel, once the most glamorous of London's railway hotels.

Euston Rd, NW1 • www.stpancras.com
• Tube: King's Cross St. Pancras

John Betjeman led a campaign to save St. Pancras in the 1960s.

British Museum

From Egyptian mummies to priceless vases and Aztec masks, London's biggest museum holds some of the world's greatest treasures.

In the British Museum's Great Court, a café and shops surround the former Reading Room.

It would take weeks to fully explore the 2.5 miles (4 km) of galleries and see even a fraction of the more than seven million ancient and modern objects owned by the British Museum, but it is possible to view the highlights in an hour or two. The majority of the collection of the oldest public museum in the world is displayed on two floors, with most of the galleries in the west wing to the left of the entrance and the larger pieces on the ground floor. Start in the jaw-dropping Great Court to get a sense of the sheer scale of the place.

GREAT COURT

The building's heart is the Great Court, designed by architect Norman Foster and opened in 2000. Once an outdoor space around the former Reading Room, it has been enclosed under a lightweight roof to create an indoor public square. There are a dozen ancient statues in the Great Court; the oldest is the head of the **Egyptian Pharaoh Amenhotep III,** from around 1400 B.C.

THE READING ROOM

The museum's circular Reading Room opened in 1857. It was here that Karl Marx wrote part of *Das Kapital,* Gandhi studied law, and Sherlock Holmes creator Sir Arthur Conan Doyle and countless other writers researched their books. When the British Library (see p. 119) opened in 1997, the Reading Room closed. Today it is used for temporary exhibits. Look up to admire the blue-and-gold-painted dome, which is made of papier-mâché.

EGYPT & NEAR EAST

Running the length of the western side of the Great Court is the Egyptian Sculpture Gallery (Room 4). Fight your way through the crowds to see the **Rosetta Stone.** This unassuming lump of rock is one

of Egyptology's most prized objects: It provided the key to understanding hieroglyphics. The stone has the same text in hieroglyphics, demotic, and ancient Greek. When it was found in 1799, the ability to read hieroglyphics had been lost for 1,400 years, but two scholars used the ancient Greek text to break the code.

From the Egyptian galleries, the massive human-headed winged bulls from the palace of King Sargon II lead to the Assyrian Galleries (Rooms 6–10). One of the highlights here are **wall reliefs** from the seventh-century B.C. Palace of Nineveh, in modern Iraq, depicting the epic drama of a royal lion hunt (Room 10).

MUMMIES & MORE

Head upstairs to see more from ancient Egypt (Rooms 61–66), where coffins and mummies—including a **mummified cat** and the **mummy of Katebet,** a woman from Thebes who died around 1300–1280 B.C. Katebet was buried wearing a wig, rings on her hands, and a scarab on her stomach that was meant to protect her in the afterlife.

■ GLORIES OF GREECE & ROME

The jewel of the museum's collection are the **Parthenon Sculptures,** known as the **Elgin Marbles** (Room 18). Created for the Parthenon in Athens, these friezes depict the struggle between humans and centaurs. Video displays show how the once brightly colored and finely carved sculptures looked when they decorated the outside of the ancient Athenian temple.

The Greek and Roman galleries continue upstairs (Rooms 69–73), with objects from domestic and ceremonial life. Decorated with mythological scenes of love, the blue-and-white Roman cameo-glass **Portland Vase** from around A.D. 525 survived being smashed by a museum visitor in 1845. Glued back together at the time, it was restored in 1987.

■ AMERICA & ASIA

The north side of the Great Court holds objects from the Americas, Asia, and the Islamic world. Artifacts here include a statue from **Easter Island** (Room 24), Native American

The fifth-century B.C. Parthenon Sculptures include dynamic groups of lifesize figures.

headdresses (Room 26), an Aztec **Turquoise Serpent** (Room 27) and masks, as well as jade, ceramics, and items from daily and ritual life.

■ TREASURES OF BRITAIN

From time to time, Britain yields up its buried treasures—often from graves or underground hiding places. The highlights on display include the greatest Anglo-Saxon treasure trove ever found—the burial hoard from **Sutton Hoo** (Room 41) excavated in 1939, the exquisitely carved **Lewis Chessmen** (Room 40), and **Lindow Man** (Room 50), whose 2,000-year-old body was found almost perfectly preserved in a peat bog. The Sutton Hoo treasure includes a rare helmet decorated with bronze and garnets. The chessmen, which came to light on Scotland's Isle of Lewis in 1831, were carved in Norway of walrus tusks and whale teeth around A.D. 1150.

■ MIDDLE EAST

In the Middle East galleries (Rooms 52–59), see an example of the world's earliest writing: **Sumerian pictographs** recording trade transactions dating from 3000 B.C.

This helmet from Sutton Hoo was reconstructed from 500 pieces.

The Sumerian Royal Graves of Ur, in modern-day Iraq, date from the mid-third millennium B.C. Many items were buried with the dead, including the **Royal Game of Ur** (Room 56), an ancient board game.

■ PRINTS & DRAWINGS

The museum has a collection of at least 50,000 drawings and more than two million prints, ranging from Renaissance to modern. Go to Room 90 to see works by Dürer, Michelangelo, Rembrandt, and Goya. The items on show rotate, but there is always something extraordinary to see.

Great Russell St., WC1 • www.britishmuseum.org • 020 7323 8299 • Closed Jan. 1 and Dec. 24–26 • Tube: Tottenham Court Road, Holborn, or Russell Square

Literary City

Opened in 1857, the British Museum Reading Room (see p. 121) put Bloomsbury at the heart of London's literary scene. Many writers have used the room, including revolutionaries Karl Marx and Vladimir Lenin, and authors Charles Dickens and Oscar Wilde. Bloomsbury isn't alone in having a literary history, so look for Blue Plaques—circular blue signs that commemorate the places where famous people lived or worked—on buildings throughout the city.

LITERARY **BLUE PLAQUES**

Agatha Christie,
58 Sheffield Terrace, W8
Daniel Defoe, 95 Stoke Newington Church St., N16
George Eliot,
3 Cheyne Walk, SW3
Ian Fleming,
22 Ebury St., SW1
Aldous Huxley,
16 Bracknell Gardens, NW3
Henry James,
34 De Vere Gardens, W8
Rudyard Kipling,
43 Villiers St., WC2
Herman Melville,
25 Craven St., WC2
George Orwell,
50 Lawford Rd., NW5
Sylvia Plath,
3 Chalcot Sq., NW1
George Bernard Shaw,
29 Fitzroy Sq., W1

Birthplace of the English Dictionary

When the British Museum first opened, the English language was still being refined. From his home at **17 Gough Square** (see p. 110), Samuel Johnson compiled the first major English dictionary between 1748 and 1759. Despite Johnson's great erudition, some blatant errors still found their way in. When asked why he had defined "pastern" as a horse's knee, rather than its foot, he replied, "ignorance madam, pure ignorance." Yet it was a great success and was considered the preeminent English dictionary for almost 200 years.

Dickensian London

Although William Shakespeare (see pp. 80–81) is lauded as England's greatest writer, Bloomsbury resident Charles Dickens is perhaps the author most associated with London. His novels buzz with the 19th-century city's sights, sounds, smells, landmarks, and teeming crowds of crossing-sweepers, servants, clerks, dressmakers, dancing

BLOOMSBURY

masters, pickpockets, prostitutes, lawyers, ladies, and baronets, all drawn in vivid detail. Many places that today look salubrious have a murky Victorian past, such as Saffron Hill in **Holborn,** where Fagin ran his den of criminals in *Oliver Twist;* **Southwark** was a warren of slums and warehouses; and notorious Seven Dials in **Covent Garden** was the haunt of petty criminals and the dirt poor. Of Dickens's many London homes, only **48 Doughty Street** *(www.dickensmuseum.com, 020 7405 2127, ££),* where he completed *The Pickwick Papers,* wrote *Oliver Twist,* and began *Nicholas Nickleby,* survives.

20th-century Bohemians

The area around the British Museum (see pp. 120–123) also gave its name to one of London's most famous literary circles: the Bloomsbury Group. Novelists Virginia Woolf and E. M. Forster, economist John Maynard Keynes, biographer Lytton Strachey, artist Roger Fry, and poet Clive Bell began meeting at **46 Gordon Square** around 1905, for "the pleasures of human intercourse and the enjoyment of beautiful objects." Their interests were wide-ranging, but they all rebelled against Victorian values, helping to shape modern attitudes to sexuality and equality.

Whereas his cat has a plinth outside his house, Samuel Johnson's statue is in nearby St. Clement Danes.

REVOLUTIONARY **WRITERS**

London has been a haven for revolutionary thinkers. Karl Marx, author of the *Communist Manifesto,* moved here in 1849, living with his family at **28 Dean Street** and working in the British Museum Reading Room. Vladimir Lenin produced his journal— *Iskra*—at 37a Clerkenwell Green, which is now home to the **Marx Memorial Library** *(www.marx-memorial-library.org, 020 7253 1485, open Mon.–Thurs., 1–2 p.m.).*

Kensington & South Kensington

Located to the west of Hyde Park, Kensington (of which South Kensington is a very distinct part) is replete with Gothic-style museum buildings, parks, gardens, and whitewashed Victorian town houses. Part of the Royal Borough of Kensington and Chelsea, the area has royal connections that go back to the 17th century. The future Queen Victoria was born in Kensington Palace in 1819. Her consort, Prince Albert, developed South Kensington into a didactic domain to enlighten Britain's masses in the 19th century. Three world-class museums are here—the Natural History Museum, the Science Museum, and the Victoria and Albert Museum—while the ornate Royal Albert Hall hosts concerts by major international orchestras and performers.

◀ **Kensington Palace's Ceremonial Dress Collection displays historic formal attire worn by members of the royal family.**

Kensington & South Kensington

*London's educational heart is filled with glorious
Victorian buildings and sumptuous parks.*

❼ Kensington Palace (see p. 134)
Members of the royal family occupy
private apartments in the palace, but
the sumptuous state rooms are open to
the public. Head west along Kensington
High Street to Holland Park.

❽ Holland Park (see
p. 135) The Kyoto Garden in
Holland Park glows with color
in fall. Leave the park by the
Ilchester Place exit, and turn
onto Holland Park Road.

**❾ Leighton House
Museum** (see p. 135)
One of London's finest
19th-century interiors
was created by artist
Frederic, Lord Leighton.

Queensway

Notting Hill
Gate

BAYSWATER ROAD

NOTTING HILL GATE

KENSINGTON CHURCH ST

PALACE GARDENS TERR

*Round
Pond*

CAMPDEN HILL

K E N S I N G T O N

❼ Kensington
Palace

ABBOTSBURY ROAD

HOLLAND
PARK

ROAD

KENSINGTON ROAD

❽

Leighton
House
Museum

STREET

High Street
Kensington

HOLLAND

ADDISON RD

HOLLAND
PARK RD.

HIGH

❾

KENSINGTON

ROAD

EARLS COURT ROAD

MARLOES RD.

WARWICK GDNS.

PEMBROKE
ROAD

CROMWELL ROAD

WARWICK ROAD

CROMWELL

EARLS

ROAD

COURT RD

CROMWELL ROAD

Gloucester
Road

E A R L S
C O U R T

S O U T H
K E N S I N G T O N

WARWICK
ROAD

Earl's
Court

OLD BROMPTON ROAD

| 0 | | 800 meters |
| 0 | | 800 yards |

**KENSINGTON & SOUTH KENSINGTON DISTANCE: 4 MILES (6.5 KM)
TIME: APPROX. 8 HOURS TUBE START: SOUTH KENSINGTON**

6 Serpentine Gallery (see p. 134)
Each summer an architect-designed temporary pavilion is erected at the east end of the gallery. Follow any path west to reach Kensington Palace.

5 Royal Albert Hall & Albert Memorial (see p. 133) The memorial to Prince Albert, Queen Victoria's consort, is close to London's preeminent concert hall. Take any path northeast to reach the Serpentine Gallery.

KENSINGTON GARDENS

Serpentine Gallery

The Serpentine

6

HYDE PARK

Albert Memorial

KNIGHTSBRIDGE

5

Royal Albert Hall

PRINCE CONSORT ROAD

EXHIBITION ROAD

QUEEN'S GATE

Science Museum

4

1

Natural History Museum

Brompton Oratory

BROMPTON ROAD

2

3

Victoria & Albert Museum

BROMPTON RD

QUEEN'S GATE

OLD BROMPTON RD

⊖ South Kensington

4 Science Museum (see pp. 132–133)
Science is made accessible with interactive displays. Head up Exhibition Road, then turn west onto Prince Consort Road and north onto Kensington Gore.

3 Brompton Oratory (see p. 131) This is London's most opulent Catholic church. Return to the V&A, then turn north on Exhibition Road.

1 Natural History Museum
(see pp. 136–137) **Start** by exploring the history of living things, from dinosaurs to Darwin. Head east on Cromwell Road.

2 Victoria and Albert Museum (see pp. 130–131)
Discover art and design, and admire items such as Tipu Sultan's tiger. Brompton Oratory is next door.

Natural History Museum

1 See pp. 136–137.

Cromwell Rd., SW7 • www.nhm.ac.uk • 020 7942 5011 • Closed
Dec. 24—26 • Tube: South Kensington

Victoria and Albert Museum

2 Enter the museum through the extravagantly carved main
entrance on Cromwell Road. On Level 1, the **Jameel Gallery,**
which displays objects from the Islamic Middle East, includes the
world's oldest dated carpet—the mid-16th-century **Ardabil Carpet.**
Measuring 34 feet by 16 feet (10.5 m by 5 m), it has a simple yet
elegant design, and it is considered one of the finest classical Persian
carpets. It adorned a Sufi shrine in the city of Ardabil in northwestern
Iran for more than 300 years. Also on Level 1 are the **Raphael
Cartoon Court,** which displays the Renaissance master's painted

The V&A's collection of plaster casts was designed as an introduction to European sculpture.

designs for tapestries for the Sistine Chapel in Rome, and the **Cast Courts.** The latter have a unique assembly of life-size plaster casts of reliefs and sculptures from Roman times to the 19th century. The star is a plaster cast of Michelangelo's masterpiece **"David."**

On Level 2, the **Medieval** and **Renaissance Galleries** explore themes such as luxury goods, printing, and enameling. Here, too, are the notebooks of 15th-century Italian polymath Leonardo da Vinci. Visitors can pore over written notes by the artist, sculptor, and inventor that contain some of his most innovative designs. The galleries also hold an exceptional collection of sculpture by the Renaissance master Donatello, including the **"Chellini Madonna"**—a carved roundel of the Virgin Mary and Child, given by the artist to his doctor in lieu of payment in 1456.

The **British Galleries 1760–1900,** on Level 4, display historic British decorative objects and furnishings. Entire rooms that were removed from demolished houses are reconstructed. Among them is the **Strawberry Room** (Room 120) in carved, painted pine—a rare example of late 18th-century Gothic Revival style.

Cromwell Rd., SW7 • www.vam.ac.uk • 020 7942 2000 • Closed Dec. 24–26 • Tube: South Kensington

Brompton Oratory

3 Marble pillars, baroque sculptures, and lofty domes make the Brompton Oratory one of London's most richly decorated buildings. Consecrated in 1884, the architect was 29-year-old Englishman Herbert Gribble, but many of the sculptures are baroque, including statues of the Twelve Apostles that were imported from Siena, Italy, and date from the 17th century. The **Lady Altar** is another 17th-century Italian import—originally created for a church in Brescia. Both composer Edward Elgar and movie director Alfred Hitchcock were married in the oratory, and KGB agents used the church as a dead-letter drop during the Cold War.

Brompton Rd., SW7 • www.bromptonoratory.com • 020 7808 0900 • Tube: South Kensington

Science Museum

4   On the ground floor, the gallery called **Making the Modern World** is dedicated to technological and scientific advances from 1750 to the present day. Here you will find the earliest steam engines, including George Stephenson's 1829 locomotive **Rocket.** Other highlights include Richard Arkwright's spinning machine of 1769, which revolutionized textile production; a sample of penicillium mold, which transformed medicine, from 1935; and the double helix model that biologists Francis Crick and James Watson used to explain the structure of DNA in 1953.

Also on the ground floor, **Exploring Space** introduces the rockets, space probes, and landers used since Sputnik 1 shot into space in 1957. One of the highlights here is an example of the J-2 rocket engine that propelled the Apollo missions toward the moon. Satellites and space debris feature in the exhibition, along with a

A 1935 airplane is one of the exhibits in the Science Museum's Making the Modern World gallery.

model of the *Eagle* lunar module in which Neil Armstrong and Buzz Aldrin touched down on the moon in 1969. For children, an interactive **Spaced Out Tour** comes with explanations of how, for example, astronauts manage in the absence of a bathroom.

Who Am I?, a completely interactive gallery on the first floor, engages visitors with exhibits that help them find out what makes each human being unique—or as they say, "What makes you you?" Find out why humans are Earth's most successful species and how memory and relationships shape identity; discover what your voice sounds like; and see how your face changes with age.

Exhibition Rd., SW7 • www.sciencemuseum.org.uk • 020 7942 4000 • Closed Dec. 24–26 • Tube: South Kensington

Royal Albert Hall & Albert Memorial

5 Its layout based on that of ancient Roman amphitheaters, the Royal Albert Hall is a magnificently decorated redbrick building famous for hosting the world's biggest annual series of classical concerts—the BBC Proms. Many rock and pop stars, such as Frank Sinatra, Bob Dylan, and Paul Simon, have also played the Albert Hall, and it was the only venue where the Beatles and the Rolling Stones ever appeared on the same bill. Facing the hall across the road in Kensington Gardens is the 180-foot-tall (55 m) **Albert Memorial,** commemorating Queen Victoria's consort, Prince Albert. An opulent canopy covers the gilded statue of the prince, while surrounding the memorial are ornately carved allegorical figures and a frieze depicting great painters, sculptors, architects, poets, and musicians.

Kensington Gore, SW7 • www.royalalberthall.com • 0845 401 5045 • Tube: South Kensington

KENSINGTON & SOUTH KENSINGTON

GOOD **EATS**

■ **BYRON (KENSINGTON)**
This is the Kensington branch of a small hamburger chain that has established a reputation for serving some of London's best Aberdeen-Angus burgers.
222 Kensington High St., W8, 020 7361 1717, £££

■ **CRÉMERIE CRÊPERIE**
Between South Kensington Tube station and the main museums, this small café serves continental breakfasts, crepes, and waffles.
2-6 Exhibition Rd., SW7, 020 7589 8947, £

■ **THE V&A CAFÉ**
London's best and oldest museum café occupies a beautiful arts-and-crafts room. Self-service counters offer a wide choice of hot food, salads, and sandwiches.
Victoria and Albert Museum, Cromwell Rd., SW7, 020 7942 2000, ££

■ **WHOLE FOODS MARKET**
In this vast emporium, you can buy food for a picnic or choose from 11 bars and four table-service restaurants.
63–97 Kensington High St., W8, 020 7368 4500, ££

Serpentine Gallery

6 A former tearoom in Kensington Gardens is now home to one of London's best galleries for contemporary art. The Serpentine Gallery holds temporary exhibitions, and it has one permanent work—a memorial to the gallery's former patron, Diana, Princess of Wales, by Ian Hamilton Finlay—set into the ground outside the entrance. The gallery has exhibited work by Gilbert & George, Damien Hurst, Andy Warhol, and Henry Moore, among others. Each summer it commissions a leading international architect to build a temporary pavilion that showcases contemporary building practices—resulting in radical and exciting structures that draw crowds.

Kensington Gardens, W2. • www.serpentinegallery.org • 020 7402 6075 • Closed between exhibitions • Tube: South Kensington

Kensington Palace

7 King William III and Queen Mary II bought the handsome redbrick mansion in 1689, and Sir Christopher Wren redesigned it to royal standards. William suffered from asthma, and the village of Kensington was far from the damp, smoky air by the Thames—and more convenient than the existing palace of Hampton Court in west London. A highlight of the palace is the **King's Staircase,** painted with figures from the court of King George I, including Peter—a feral child from the woods of Germany—and the king's Polish page, Ulric. The stairs lead to the **state apartments** and the **royal bedrooms,** where Queen Victoria was born in 1819 and was told of her accession to the throne 18 years later. More recently, Kensington Palace was the marital home of Charles and Diana, Prince and Princess of Wales; after they divorced, Diana stayed here until her death in 1997. The **Sunken Gardens** are based on those at **Hampton Court.** The grounds have been extensively restored to provide terraces and a café in the **Orangery.**

Kensington Gardens, W8 • www.hrp.org.uk • 0844 482 7777 • ££££ • Closed Dec. 24–26 • Tube: High Street Kensington or Queensway

Holland Park

8 This peaceful 55-acre (22 ha) park, reached from the western end of Kensington High Street, is one of London's most romantic green spaces. At its center are the remains of **Holland House,** a large Jacobean mansion built in 1605 and mostly destroyed by World War II bombs, which now houses a youth hostel. Each summer, a huge tent beside Holland House provides the setting for a season of opera. The park is home to strutting peacocks, whose shrill cries reverberate around a series of gardens, including the graceful **Kyoto Garden,** laid out with Japanese plants and features. The café serves snacks all day, and the **Orangery** and the **Ice House** show temporary art exhibitions. For families, the park also offers one of London's best children's adventure playgrounds.

Enter the park on Kensington High St., W8 • www.operahollandpark.com
• Tube: Kensington (Olympia), High Street Kensington, or Holland Park

Leighton House Museum

9 Victorian artist Frederic, Lord Leighton (1830–1896) built this exotic mansion on a quiet Kensington side street. The centerpiece is the **Arab Hall,** covered with some of the thousands of tiles—including Iznik tiles, noted for their dazzling blue—that Leighton brought back from the Ottoman Empire, along with wooden lattice screens from Syria and Egypt. Leighton (the first artist to be made a lord) spent the 30 years he lived here turning the house into a palace of art, filling it with sculptures and some 80 oil paintings of his own, as well as paintings by the Pre-Raphaelites, several of whom were friends.

12 Holland Park Rd., W14 • www.rbkc.gov.uk • 020 7602 3316 • ££ • Closed Tues., Jan. 1–2 and Dec. 25–28 • Tube: Kensington (Olympia) or Holland Park

A cat peers up at a peacock in one of the mosaics that line Leighton House's exquisite Arab Hall.

Natural History Museum

Cathedral-like galleries make a fitting home for the world's largest, most fascinating natural history collection.

A model skeleton of a *Diplodocus* dinosaur dominates the majestic Central Hall.

From the massive—including numerous dinosaur fossils—to the microscopic, the collections of the Natural History Museum comprise more than 70 million specimens. Here you will find everything from the restored skull of a dodo– among the few surviving remains of the ill-fated bird—to a full-size model of a blue whale to early human fossils. Completed in the 1880s, the building itself is a masterpiece of neo-Romanesque architecture. It is divided into four zones—Green, Blue, Red, and Orange—each with a different focus.

■ GREEN ZONE

This zone, including the Central Hall, presents an overview of the planet's ecology. Highlights include a **Creepy Crawlies gallery,** marine fossils, and bird specimens, from *Archaeopteryx*— the earliest known bird—to modern hummingbirds. On Floor 1, see a copy of the tiny skeleton of five-million-year-old **"Lucy,"** one of the first humanlike creatures to walk upright.

■ BLUE ZONE

This ground-floor area to the left of the Central Hall has a major dinosaur gallery dominated by a *Triceratops* **skeleton** and an animatronic model of a *Tyrannosaurus rex,* complete with 6-inch-long (15 cm) teeth. In the mammals gallery you can inspect a suspended model of a blue whale— larger than any dinosaur.

■ RED ZONE

Reached via a side entrance on Exhibition Road, this zone focuses on the forces that shape the Earth. On view are one of the planet's oldest rocks (dating back around 3.85 billion years), fluorescent minerals, and a piece of moon rock brought back

SAVVY **TRAVELER**

In a tucked-away corner of the Green Zone, the **Vault** displays a sparkling array of gemstones, metals, and meteorites. The stars of the collection include naturally colored diamonds and the Nakhla meteorite, a meteorite from Mars that fell to Earth in Egypt in 1911.

by the Apollo 16 mission. On the mezzanine is an interactive **Earth Lab,** with staff on hand to answer questions. On Floor 2, watch footage of volcanic eruptions and step inside a simulator mimicking the effects of the 1995 Kobe earthquake on a supermarket.

■ ORANGE ZONE

Enter this zone via the Blue Zone. Its state-of-the-art **Darwin Centre** is built in the shape of a cocoon. Take the elevator to Floor 7, then descend a walkway that allows you to view hundreds of plant and insect specimens. You can also take part in interactive activities and see scientists at work. Back on the ground floor, visit the **Attenborough Studio** to watch films, talk with staff, and handle live specimens, such as a python or tarantula.

Cromwell Rd., SW7 • www.nhm.ac.uk • 020 7942 5011 • Closed Dec. 24–26
• Tube: South Kensington

Parks & Gardens

The Royal Parks owe their existence to the stubborn resolve of successive monarchs to hunt game even when residing in their urban palaces. Large, rural retreats were supplemented in the 19th century by newly created urban parks and legally protected areas of undeveloped wasteland (heath) and woodland. The population density of London is half that of Paris or New York thanks to the generous supply of green spaces.

Equestrians use Rotten Row (above) in Hyde Park. In St. James's Park (right), the view east along the lake offers a glimpse of William Kent's Horse Guards building.

Royal Parks

In medieval times, when London was confined within city walls, much of what is now the metropolis was forest. Hunting was a popular pursuit and one that kings were loath to abandon as the city grew. In 1532, King Henry VIII confiscated the area now occupied by **St. James's Park** from Westminster Abbey and stocked it with deer and other game for his own amusement. Four years later, the king took over the manor of Hyde and added it to his hunting ground to form what is now **Hyde Park.** Farther out, **Richmond Park** and **Greenwich Park** were enclosed in the 15th and 17th centuries respectively.

King Charles I was the first monarch to open the Royal Parks to the public, admitting his subjects to Hyde Park in 1637. In 1730, Queen Caroline, wife of King George II, initiated the creation of the sinuous **Serpentine lake** at the heart of Hyde Park. She also directed the laying out of **Kensington Gardens** on the western side of the Serpentine. In 1872, an act of Parliament designated the northeast tip of Hyde Park as a place where people could stand up and express their views, however subversive, and the spot became known as **Speaker's Corner.** In the southwest of the park, the **Diana, Princess of Wales Memorial Fountain,** designed by American Kathryn Gustafson, is a popular destination.

Parks for the People

Municipal parks were first created in the Victorian era in response to overcrowded conditions in the rapidly expanding city. The first to open was **Victoria Park** in the East End in 1841. Elsewhere wide stretches of heath and woods were saved from the builders as the city grew. Most famous of these is **Hampstead Heath,** which, with its mix of sporting activities, walking trails, quiet corners, and cultural events typifies London's open spaces.

PARK
PERFORMANCES

Holland Park Holds an open-air opera season each summer. **Kensington High Street or Holland Park, W8, www.operahollandpark.com**

Hyde Park Music events, including the Hard Rock Calling and Wireless festivals, feature world-famous acts. **Hyde Park, W2, www.royalparks.gov.uk**

Regents Park The open-air theater stages plays through the summer. **Regents Park, NW1, www.royalparks.gov.uk**

Victoria Park Music events take place on summer weekends, Hackney, E9, www.tower hamlets.gov.uk

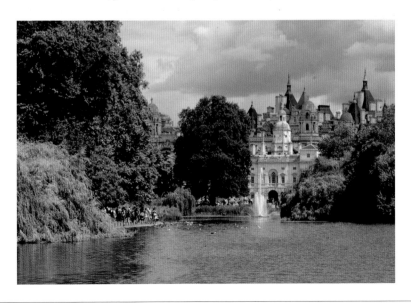

Afternoon Tea

Served between 3 and 5 p.m., afternoon tea can be a luxurious event, involving delicate china and fanned napkins as well as the culinary essentials of exquisite teas, dainty cakes, and elegant sandwiches. It is a quintessentially English tradition for which London is famous, perfect before a trip to the theater.

■ HIGH CLASS TEAS

To take tea in a royal home, visit Kensington Palace's 18th-century **Orangery** (*Kensington Palace, W8, 020 3166 6112, ££*), where you choose from more than ten flavors of tea, served with homemade cakes and sandwiches.

The official tea sommelier at **The Lanesborough** (*Hyde Park Corner, SW1, 020 7259 5599, ££££*) will help you select among exotic options like Dragon Well green tea or Wild Tuo Cha, aged for 17 years to concentrate its flavor. **The Goring** (*Beeston Pl., SW1, 020 7396 9000, ££££*) in Victoria offers traditional English teatime fare, notably freshly baked scones with Devonshire clotted cream and jam.

Both the **Ritz** (*150 Piccadilly, W1, 020 7300 2345, ££££*) and, in Mayfair, **Brown's Hotel** (*Albemarle St., W15, 020 7493 6020, ££££*) serve dainty sandwiches, scones, and cakes from three-tiered cake stands—with Champagne if you are feeling extravagant. At Brown's, you can schedule a tea-torial to learn sugary secrets from the house pastry chef. Also in Mayfair, the **Connaught's** (*Carlos Pl., W1, 020 7107 8861, ££££*) "Chic and Shock" afternoon tea adds just a few haute gourmet twists to the tradition, including raspberry and violet jam, and smoked-salmon-with-wasabi-cream finger sandwiches.

■ MUSEUM TEA ROOMS

Tea at the **National Gallery** (*Trafalgar Sq., WC2, 020 7747 5942, ££*) is an utterly British experience, with local ingredients and homemade preserves. Next door you can have tea on the top floor of the **National Portrait Gallery** (*St. Martin's Pl., WC2, 020 7312 2490, ££*) with panoramic views over London. The **Wallace Collection** (*Manchester Sq., W1, 020 7563 9505, ££*), in Marylebone, displays some of

Scones, jam tarts, and a cream-filled sponge cake are regular components of afternoon tea.

the best French paintings, porcelain, and furniture anywhere outside of France. The afternoon tea is also distinctly French, featuring foie gras, salmon tartare, and French pastries.

■ TRENDY TEAS

Londoners book weeks in advance to experience Piccadilly's **Sketch** (*9 Conduit St., W1, 020 7659 4500, £££*), a concept space dedicated to both art and food. But no reservations are taken at the more casual Parlour gallery, which serves afternoon tea. Enjoy colorful macaroons while keeping an eye open for lounging fashionistas. For something even less traditional and equally fashionable, try afternoon "Cocktails and Cupcakes" at Mayfair's **The May Fair** (*Stratton St., W1, 020 7915 3894, £££*). It may not be tea for the family, but it is hard to pass up the bar's tea-inspired cocktails and paired cupcakes.

■ GREAT VALUE TEAS

With its floral wallpaper, **Bea's of Bloomsbury** (*44 Theobalds Rd., WC1, 020 7242 8330, ££*) is a baking paradise devoted to colorful cupcakes and delightfully dense brownies—and they also serve a wonderful afternoon tea, at a fraction of the cost of the big hotels.

CHELSEA,
BELGRAVIA, &
KNIGHTSBRIDGE

CHELSEA, BELGRAVIA, & KNIGHTSBRIDGE

Chelsea, Belgravia, & Knightsbridge

These three neighborhoods are home to some of London's wealthiest people. The streets abound with chic boutiques and opulent department stores, including Harrods, London's most exclusive emporium. This luxurious consumption is juxtaposed with elegant churches, a hospital for military veterans, and a 17th-century garden dedicated to the healing powers of plants. In Victorian times, Chelsea was an artists' quarter, and the works of many of its residents—including Whistler, Rossetti, and Turner—can be seen in Tate Britain. Today, it is the Saatchi Gallery that sets the artistic pace with its exhibitions of contemporary art. Literary figures lived here, too: Visit the home of social critic Thomas Carlyle, known as the "sage of Chelsea."

144 Neighborhood Walk

152 In Depth: Tate Britain

154 Distinctly London: Caught on Canvas

156 Best Of: Designer Knightsbridge

❶ **Swinging Sixties music idols such as Jimi Hendrix and the Rolling Stones were aficionados of the Chelsea Potter pub on King's Road.**

LONDON'S NEIGHBORHOODS | **143**

Chelsea, Belgravia, & Knightsbridge

Combine high-end shopping in Knightsbridge with visits to galleries and churches, and enjoy a quiet interlude in the Chelsea Physic Garden.

❶ Harrods (see pp. 146–147) **Start at** London's flagship store, where luxury pervades. On leaving, walk east on Brompton Road and Knightsbridge, then turn right onto Wilton Place.

❾ Carlyle's House (see p. 151) **Visit the** home of the Victorian writer Thomas Carlyle, one of the many former local residents who gave Chelsea its literary and artistic character.

❽ Chelsea Old Church (see p. 151) A statue of St. Thomas More, erected in 1969, stands outside the church near his home. Return east on Cheyne Walk and turn left onto Cheyne Row.

Map labels: Hyde Park Corner · St. Paul's Church, Knightsbridge · KNIGHTSBRIDGE · Knightsbridge · BELGRAVIA SQUARE · Harrods · BROMPTON ROAD · BEAUCHAMP PL · PONT STREET · SLOANE · BROMPTON RD. · South Kensington · SLOANE STREET · Sloane Square · Gloucester Road · ONSLOW SQ. · SLOANE AVENUE · The Saatchi Gallery · OLD BROMPTON ROAD · FULHAM ROAD · SYDNEY STREET · KING'S ROAD · CHELTENHAM TERRACE · CHELSEA · SOUTH KENSINGTON · OLD CHURCH STREET · FLOOD STREET · ROYAL HOSPITAL RD. · Royal Hospital Chelsea · RANELAGH GARDENS · Carlyle's House · OAKLEY STREET · CHELSEA EMBANKMENT · CHELSEA PHYSIC GARDEN · Chelsea Old Church · ALBERT BRIDGE

0 — 800 meters
0 — 800 yards

**CHELSEA, BELGRAVIA, & KNIGHTSBRIDGE DISTANCE: 6 MILES (9.6 KM)
TIME: APPROX. 8.5 HOURS TUBE START: KNIGHTSBRIDGE**

② St. Paul's Church, Knightsbridge (see p. 147) The Victorian church's plain facade belies a rich interior. Take the tube from Hyde Park Corner to Pimlico.

WESTMINSTER

VENOR PLACE

N SQUARE

ECCLESTON ST

Victoria

Victoria Station

LGRAVIA

ECCLESTON BRIDGE

ECCLESTON BRIDGE ROAD

BUCKINGHAM PALACE ROAD

BELGRAVE

WAY

ROAD

WARWICK

ROCHESTER ROW

VAUXHALL BRIDGE ROAD

HORSEFERRY ROAD

MARSHAM ST.

LAMBETH BRIDGE

③ Tate Britain

Tate Britain

PIMLICO

Pimlico

MILLBANK

GROSVENOR ROAD

VAUXHALL BRIDGE

Thames

CHELSEA BRIDGE

GE ROAD

BRIDGE RD

③ Tate Britain (see pp. 152–153) View the best of British art from the 16th century until today. Take the Tube from Pimlico to Sloane Square.

④ Saatchi Gallery (see p. 148) Expect a few surprises at reclusive advertising guru Charles Saatchi's contemporary art gallery, then stroll west on King's Road.

⑤ King's Road (see p. 148) Running southwest from Sloane Square, Chelsea's main thoroughfare never goes out of fashion. Turn south onto Cheltenham Terrace toward Royal Hospital Road.

⑦ Chelsea Physic Garden (see p. 150) Founded by the ancient Company of Apothecaries, the garden is a showcase for healing plants. On leaving, turn left on Royal Hospital Road and continue west on Chelsea Embankment to Old Church Street.

⑥ Royal Hospital Chelsea (see p. 149) Visit the home of scarlet-coated Chelsea Pensioners, which is also the site of the annual Chelsea Flower Show, then continue west on Royal Hospital Road.

Harrods

Emblazoned with the motto "All Things for All People Everywhere," Harrods has been supplying luxury goods and services to a wealthy worldwide clientele for more than a century. From a one-room grocery shop founded by Charles Henry Harrod in 1849, the business has expanded into high-end fashion, perfumes, luxury food, electronics, jewelry, furniture, stationery, gifts, kitchen appliances, sports equipment (including golf carts), and even rabbits, gerbils, and puppies. You can have a suit made to order or engage a personal shopper. Doormen attired in trademark olive-green livery usher customers across the threshold but turn away anyone not considered appropriately dressed. Inside, glittering displays vie for attention in hundreds of departments on seven floors. The highlight is the **Food Hall**—a confection of tilework and mosaic friezes by 19th-century sculptor W. J. Neatby—where

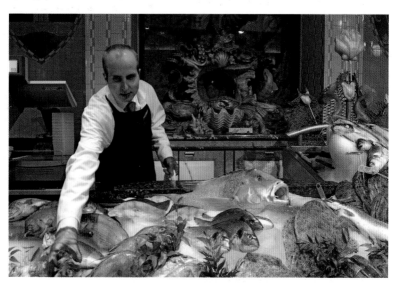

Harrods' Food Hall tempts shoppers with an assortment of fish, oysters, and caviar.

artistically displayed meat and fish, patisseries, fruit, and vegetables tingle the tastebuds. Aside from the Food Hall, there are more than **30 other eateries,** from the ground-floor Parisian tearoom to the fifth-floor Georgian restaurant. Another must-see sight is the **Egyptian Hall,** festooned with statues and art mimicking ancient Egypt, where former Harrods owner Mohammed Al-Fayed built a shrine to his son Dodi and Princess Diana, who died together in 1997.

87–135 Brompton Rd., SW1 • www.harrods.com • 020 7730 1234 • Closed Easter Sun. and Dec. 25–27 • Tube: Knightsbridge

St. Paul's Church, Knightsbridge

2 The parish church of Knightsbridge is celebrated as much for its parishioners as for its high Victorian style. The 1st Duke of Wellington (1769–1852), vanquisher of Napoleon, who lived on nearby Hyde Park Corner, was a regular worshiper in the church's early days. Today's celebrities may be seen at the Christmas carol service. St. Paul's was built in 1843 with a fashionably plain facade that belies a richly decorated interior. Elegant cast-iron pillars support galleries on three sides. George Frederick Bodley, a specialist in the Gothic Revival style, designed the reredos behind the altar and the carved rood screen separating the nave from the chancel, both of which were added in 1892. On the walls of the nave, tiled panels by Daniel Bell (1870s) depicting the life of Christ are interspersed with scenes from the crucifixion by Gerald Moira (1920s). Throughout, paintings and statues of people connected with the history of St. Paul's are on view.

32a Wilton Pl., SW1 • www.stpaulsknightsbridge.org • 020 7201 9999 • Tube: Knightsbridge or Hyde Park Corner

GOOD **EATS**

■ **CAFFÉ FRATELLI**
Sit outside and imbibe Chelsea life on a square off King's Road. Italian fare features pastas, paninis, and good cappuccinos. **10 Duke of York Sq., SW3, 020 7823 6800, £**

■ **THE GRENADIER**
Once the Grenadier Guards' officers' mess, the mews pub brims with military souvenirs. Snack on sandwiches in the bar or eat in the restaurant. **18 Wilton Row, SW1, 020 7235 3074, £££**

■ **HARVEY NICHOLS**
Start the day with a full English breakfast or freshly squeezed juice and pastries at the Fifth Floor Café and Terrace. Lunch, tea, and dinner are also served. **109–125 Knightsbridge, SW1, 020 7823 1839, £££** (see p. 156)

Tate Britain

3 See pp. 152–153.

Millbank, SW1 • www.tate.org.uk • 020 7887 8888 • Closed Dec. 24—26
• Visitors wishing to see particular works should call in advance • Tube: Pimlico

Saatchi Gallery

4 They may be thought-provoking, controversial, even outrageous, but the exhibitions at one of Britain's leading galleries for contemporary art are never uninteresting. Founded by art collector and advertising magnate Charles Saatchi, the current gallery occupies a former army headquarters, whose airy white rooms give the artworks and installations space to shine. Most impressive is Richard Wilson's **"20:50,"** a steel container half-filled with oil to create a reflective black lake, in Room 13. Visitors can enter the room via a walkway. The gallery has exhibited pioneering 20th-century artists such as Jeff Koons, Tracey Emin, and Damien Hirst, and new talent is often showcased.

King's Rd., SW3 • www.saatchi-gallery.co.uk • 020 7811 3070 • Tube: Sloane Square

IN **THE KNOW**

In 1764, eight-year-old Wolfgang Amadeus Mozart composed his first symphony while staying at **180 Ebury Street**, just a few streets south of King's Road. The building is marked with a plaque.

King's Road

5 The Swinging Sixties brought boutiques and psychedelia to the King's Road. Since then, gentrification has changed the style, but the street has retained its reputation for stylish shopping. In Sloane Square the **Royal Court Theatre** (*Sloane Sq., www. royalcourttheatre.com, 020 7565 5000*) challenges audiences with its avant-garde productions, while clothing boutiques such as punk fashion designer Vivienne Westwood's **World's End** (*430 King's Rd., www.worldsendshop. co.uk, 020 7352 6551*) and interior design stores are interspersed with pubs and restaurants along the King's Road itself.

King's Rd., between Sloane Sq. and Waterford Rd. • www.kingsroad.co.uk
• Tube: Sloane Square

Formal dress for Chelsea Pensioners is based on an 18th-century British Army uniform.

Royal Hospital Chelsea

This stately 17th-century redbrick building designed by Sir Christopher Wren "for the succor and relief of veterans broken by age and war" is still home to British Army veterans known as Chelsea Pensioners. A golden statue by Grinling Gibbons of King Charles II forms the centerpiece of the central **Figure Court.** The **Chapel** and the large porticoed entrance to the **Great Hall** where the pensioners dine dominate one side of the immaculate court and the Long Wards, where they sleep in wainscoted berths, forms the other two sides. You can see a mock-up of their berths in the hospital's small **museum.** In spring, the grounds are transformed into gardens for the annual Chelsea Flower Show.

Royal Hospital Rd., SW3 • www.chelsea-pensioners.org.uk • 020 7881 5200 • Closed Sat., Sun., bank holidays, and for hospital events • Groups of up to 10 people can visit (but not view the Long Wards) 10 a.m.–12 a.m. and 2 p.m.–4 p.m. • Tube: Sloane Square

Chelsea Physic Garden

Sheltered behind high walls, this 4-acre (1.6 ha) garden was founded for medicinal research and education by the Society of Apothecaries in 1673. Many of the plants nurtured here have contributed to the development of commonly used drugs, such as aspirin, which was derived from the meadowsweet herb. Plants like this can be seen in the **Pharmaceutical Garden,** while the **Garden of World Medicine** features healing plants favored by tribal communities. Flowers used in perfumes and aromatherapy are on show throughout the garden. The shop sells plants and, from August to September, honey from its bees.

66 Royal Hospital Rd., SW3 • www.chelseaphysicgarden.co.uk • 020 7352 5646 • ££ • Closed Sat, Mon., and Nov.–March • Tube: Sloane Square

Sir Hans Sloane provided the land for the Chelsea Physic Garden, and his statue keeps watch there.

Chelsea Old Church

8 Although the restored redbrick exterior creates the impression that this is a modern church, the building actually dates from the 13th century and is reportedly the place where King Henry VIII married his third wife, Jane Seymour, in 1536. The church includes a chapel that was rebuilt by Henry's onetime advisor and lord chancellor, Sir Thomas More, who lived close by. **More's Chapel** was one of the few parts of the church to survive bomb damage in World War II. A group of rare books, including a Bible from 1717, a 1723 prayer book, and a Homilies from 1683, also survived and are the only **chained books** in a London church—the practice of chaining books to shelves or reading desks was a way of preventing theft in a time when books were rare and valuable.

2 Old Church St., SW3 • www.chelseaoldchurch.org.uk • 020 7795 1019 • Tube: South Kensington or Sloane Square

Carlyle's House

9 The Scottish writer and historian Thomas Carlyle was one of Victorian London's foremost men of letters. He was known as "the sage of Chelsea," and many notable guests, including author Charles Dickens, novelist George Eliot, philosopher John Stuart Mill, poet Alfred Lord Tennyson, and naturalist Charles Darwin, visited. Carlyle also wrote many of his best known books here, including *The French Revolution,* which he had to write a second time since the first copy was accidentally burnt by Mill's maid. In 1895, only 14 years after his death, Carlyle's home was opened to the public and has been kept how it was when he lived here. The building dates from the early 18th century and sits on one of London's best preserved Georgian streets. Inside are paintings by American artist James McNeill Whistler, as well as books, furniture, and personal effects belonging to Carlyle and his wife, Jane—herself a prominent essayist. A highlight is Carlyle's much loved garden, including a fig tree that still produces fruit.

24 Cheyne Row, SW3 • www.nationaltrust.org.uk • 020 7352 7087 • ££ • Closed Mon., Tues., and Nov.–Feb. • Tube: Sloane Square or South Kensington

SAVVY **TRAVELER**

For antiques and art, head to **Pimlico Road,** just south of Sloane Square, which has a large choice of specialty shops selling everything from 17th-century paintings to art deco furniture.

Tate Britain

The original Tate gallery is dedicated to the work of British artists and artists resident in Britain.

Tate Britain has the world's largest collection of J. M. W. Turner's work, including "The Blue Rigi."

From the formal charm of 16th-century Tudor portraits to the sometimes controversial work of contemporary artists, Tate Britain traces the story of more than 500 years of British art. The main galleries are arranged chronologically and thematically and are interspersed with small temporary exhibits. The Artist Rooms series shows work by contemporary artists on a rotating basis, and the gallery changes its displays regularly to provide fresh perspectives on the work on view.

■ WILLIAM BLAKE

Tate Britain owns many works by this 18th-century visionary artist and poet, who illustrated his own poems and those of others, such as Dante and Milton. Seek out Blake's **"Newton,"** an attack on scientific reason that shows the great scientist facing into the darkness. Poems from his "Songs of Innocence and of Experience," such as **"Tyger,"** are shown in their original, illustrated form.

■ MASTER OF LIGHT & ATMOSPHERE

The **Clore Wing** is devoted to J. M. W. Turner, including his oil paintings, watercolors, and drawings. Check out his late paintings, such as **"Sunrise with Sea Monsters"** (circa 1845), in which forms dissolve in shimmering light. An exhibit follows Turner's experiments in printmaking and watercolor.

■ 19TH-CENTURY AVANT-GARDE

Pre-Raphaelite painters such as Dante Gabriel Rossetti, William Holman Hunt, and John Everett Millais wished to revitalize painting using intense colors and a profusion of naturalistic detail. They espoused literary and mythical subjects; Millais's **"Ophelia,"**

depicting the drowning Shakespearean heroine, is a perennial favorite.

■ FROM PEACE TO WAR

In the displays spanning the pre-World War I period through to the 1950s, John Singer Sargent's pretty **"Carnation, Lily, Lily, Rose"** contrasts with Mark Gertler's **"Merry-Go-Round,"** an image of World War I's horror, and Francis Bacon's fractured forms in **"Three Studies for Figures at the Base of a Crucifixion,"** painted in 1944.

■ BRITART

Tate Britain's holdings of contemporary art include work by Young British Artists, such as Damien Hirst and Sarah Lucas, who emerged in the 1980s, and the more senior Gilbert & George, whose **"Red Morning Trouble"** (1977) consists of photographs of both artists alternating with river views.

CHELSEA, BELGRAVIA, & KNIGHTSBRIDGE

Millbank, SW1 • www.tate.org.uk • 020 7887 8888 • Closed Dec. 24–26 • Visitors wishing to see a particular work should call in advance to check if it is on display • Tube: Pimlico

Caught on Canvas

Portrait painters, landscape artists, French Impressionists—all have been inspired by London and its people over the centuries, creating a vast archive of the city's changing face. Van Dyck painted King Charles I, Canaletto captured the city's pageantry and architecture, Whistler the waterside, and Turner the Houses of Parliament. Today, London shines at the cutting edge of contemporary art.

Hogarth & Turner

Two of London's best known artists are William Hogarth and J. M. W Turner. Hogarth was a satirist who often portrayed the less salubrious side of the city, for example "A Rake's Progress" (circa 1735), which depicts gambling dens and brothels in a sobering story of fecklessness and corruption.

In the 19th century, romantic landscape artist Turner was fascinated by weather and light effects, which can be seen in his numerous impressionistic watercolor studies of the dramatic burning of the Houses of Parliament in 1834.

Artists from Abroad

Many foreign artists have been drawn to London, often for royal patronage. In the 16th century, German portrait painter Hans Holbein found favor with King Henry VIII, and a century later, baroque artists Peter Paul Rubens and Anthony van Dyck were both knighted by King Charles I.

The cityscape has also inspired. Venetian artist Canaletto painted the River Thames 48 times in the 1750s, and American James McNeill Whistler was also taken with the river when he moved to London in 1859. So was Claude Monet, who painted the smoggy Thames at Westminster during a stay in London in 1870–1871. The view lured him back again in 1899–1901, resulting in his "Houses of Parliament" series.

Contemporary Viewpoint

In the early 1990s, the city's art scene began making its presence felt in East London's Spitalfields, Shoreditch, and Hoxton. The duo Gilbert & George predate the arrival of younger artists in the area, having lived close to Brick Lane for more than 30 years. Their "Twenty London East One Pictures" of 2004–2005 ranged rows of street names of their own E1 postcode around images of their gesticulating selves—an unexpected piece for a cluster of streets that were once no-go areas.

CHELSEA, BELGRAVIA, & KNIGHTSBRIDGE

ARTIST'S **HOMES**

John Constable (1776–1837) 40 Well Walk, NW3

Vincent van Gogh (1853–1890) 87 Hackford Road, SW9

Dante Gabriel Rossetti (1828–1882) 110 Hallam Street, W1

J. M. W. Turner (1775–1851) 40 Sandycombe Road, TW1

James McNeill Whistler (1834–1903) 96 Cheyne Walk, SW10

Whistler would often paint scenes from memory in his Chelsea studio (above). The mist in this (left) and Monet's other London paintings was actually smog, which blighted the city at that time.

Designer Knightsbridge

Dazzling boutiques and designer shops located near the upscale Harrods and Harvey Nichols stores provide some serious shopping opportunities for Knightsbridge's extremely wealthy residents. Local British designers, classic Italian names, and specialists for accessories and shoes are all represented.

■ HARRODS

London's flagship store (see pp. 146–147) has a wide selection of designer labels, including Diane von Furstenberg, Britt Lintner, Piazza Sempione, Liu Jo, Robert Rodriguez, Lee Klabin, Elizabeth Hurley, Ted Baker, Tory Burch, and many others.

■ HARVEY NICHOLS

Many local people choose not to face the crowds at Harrods and instead enjoy shopping at "Harvey Nicks," a chic alternative with eight floors of designer collections and a huge beauty department. The store originally opened as a linen shop in 1813 and still includes an impressive range of home products. The top level features a restaurant, bar, café, and food market.

109–125 Knightsbridge, SW1 • www.harvey nichols.com • 0845 604 1888 • Closed Easter Sun. and Dec. 25 • Tube: Knightsbridge

■ SLOANE STREET BOUTIQUES

If the big department stores are overwhelming, enjoy the intimacy of smaller boutiques dedicated to famous designers such as **Giorgio Armani** (37–42 Sloane St., SW1) and **Nicole Fahri** (193 Sloane St., SW1). A short stroll along Sloane Street offers **Dior** (31 Sloane St., SW1), **Chanel** (167–170 Sloane St., SW1), **Prada** (43–45 Sloane St., SW1), **Gucci** (18 Sloane St., SW1), **Alberta Ferretti** (205–206 Sloane St., SW1), and **Katharine Hamnett** (20 Sloane St., SW1) to name a few. These smaller shops often have exclusive products from the latest collections. There are also some exquisite lingerie shops here, such as **La Perla** (163 Sloane St., SW1) which specializes in elegant Italian designs, and around the corner, **Rigby and Peller** (2 Hans Road, SW3), which supplies underwear to the royal family.

Sloane Street has become London's top shopping district, with designer stores such as Prada.

■ BRITISH DESIGNS

Watch for British brands such as **Burberry** *(2 Brompton Rd., SW1)*, famous for its tartan pattern and iconic trench coat. **Jo Malone** *(150 Sloane St., SW1)* is loved for its luxury fragrances for the home, bath, and body. **Paul Smith's** Women's Collection *(84–86 Sloane Ave., SW3)* relies on simplicity, with a mix of quintessential British style and a modern edge, and **Lulu Guinness** *(3 Ellis St., SW1)* offers unique handbags and accessories in a 1950s style. **Gwendolyn Carrie** *(4 Ellis St., SW1)* supplies handcrafted shoes made with fish-skin leather.

■ SHOES

Strap on your Jimmy Choos or stomp along in your Church's Oxfords to find a few extra pairs of shoes. Check out the ageless **Church's** *(143 Brompton Rd., SW1)*, beloved by grandfathers, while **Russell & Bromley** *(45 and 77 Brompton Rd., SW1)* provides classic, stylish shoes for men and women. Or choose from the amazing Italians, **Botega Veneta** *(33 Sloane St., SW1)*, **Salvatore Ferragamo** *(207 Sloane St., SW1)*, or **Fratelli Rossetti** *(196 Sloane St., SW1)*. And, of course, pick up a pair of **Jimmy Choos** *(32 Sloane St., SW1)*.

EAST
LONDON

Thames

East London

Traditionally home of dockworkers and immigrants, East London is Britain's capital at its multicultural best and holds some of its most vibrant attractions. The Tower of London has been England's most important fortress (and prison) for almost a thousand years and is still charged with protecting the Crown Jewels. Close by is Tower Bridge, where you can take its high-level walk across the Thames for panoramic river views. If you're lucky, you may see the bridge open below for a ship to pass through. A Tube stop north brings you to the Whitechapel, one of London's leading contemporary art galleries. Nearby, Brick Lane is the center of the capital's alternative scene. Here you'll find street art vintage fashion boutiques, curry houses, and the city's coolest Sunday market. Farther east, Canary Wharf's gleaming office towers rise above the revitalized Docklands area. Opposite, at Greenwich on the south bank of the Thames, the tea clipper *Cutty Sark,* the Old Royal Naval College, and the National Maritime Museum evoke London's maritime past.

❶ **The Yeoman Warders and the colony of ravens are popular attractions at the Tower of London.**

East London

*Discover history, elegance, and culture
in a Thames-side setting.*

EAST LONDON

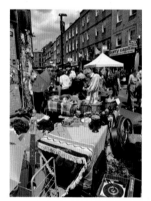

④ Brick Lane (see pp. 163–164) Home to successive waves of immigrants, Brick Lane is vibrant, quirky, and chic, and has one of the capital's best street markets. Take the Docklands Light Railway (DLR) from Tower Gateway to West India Quay or Canary Wharf.

❸ Whitechapel Gallery (see p. 163) In the heart of the East End, the gallery has temporary exhibitions of modern art. Go left out of the gallery and head east on Whitechapel High Street, then turn north onto Osborn Street.

❷ Tower Bridge (see pp. 162–163) Explore the bridge and take in the views from the upper walkways. Take the Tube from Tower Hill to Aldgate East.

❶ Tower of London (see pp. 168–169) The original keep was constructed by William the Conqueror. Walk around to Tower Bridge Approach.

**EAST LONDON   DISTANCE: 7.7 MILES (12 KM)
TIME: APPROX. 9 HOURS   TUBE START: TOWER HILL**

HACKNEY

HOMERTO

KINGSLAND ROAD

BETHNAL GREE

Bethna
Green

Shoreditch High Street

Stepney
Green

Whitechapel

MILE EN

STEPNE

Whitechapel
Art Gallery

WHITECHAPEL

BRICK LN

WHITECHAPEL RD

Aldgate East

Aldgate

COMMERCIAL ROA

Tower
Gateway

WAPPING

Tower Hill

Shadwel

Tower of
London

ROTHERHITHE
TUNNEL

Tower
Bridge

St.
Katharine
Docks

Wapping

Thames

Rotherhithe

Bermondsey

Canada
Water

Surrey Quays

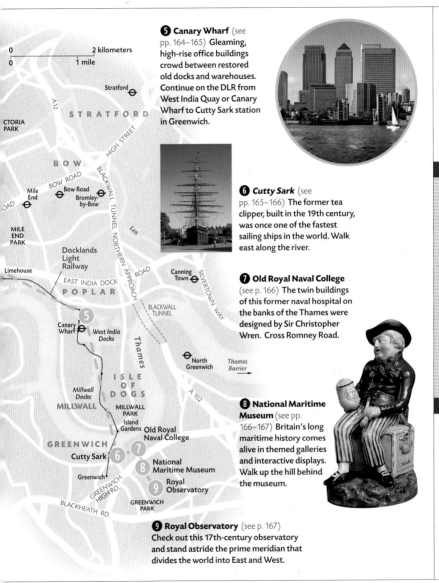

5 Canary Wharf (see pp. 164–165) Gleaming, high-rise office buildings crowd between restored old docks and warehouses. Continue on the DLR from West India Quay or Canary Wharf to Cutty Sark station in Greenwich.

6 Cutty Sark (see pp. 165–166) The former tea clipper, built in the 19th century, was once one of the fastest sailing ships in the world. Walk east along the river.

7 Old Royal Naval College (see p. 166) The twin buildings of this former naval hospital on the banks of the Thames were designed by Sir Christopher Wren. Cross Romney Road.

8 National Maritime Museum (see pp. 166–167) Britain's long maritime history comes alive in themed galleries and interactive displays. Walk up the hill behind the museum.

9 Royal Observatory (see p. 167) Check out this 17th-century observatory and stand astride the prime meridian that divides the world into East and West.

Tower of London

1 See pp. 168–169.

Tower of London, Tower Hill, EC3 • www.hrp.org.uk/toweroflondon
• 0844 482 7777 • £££££ • Closed Jan. 1 and Dec. 24–26 • Tube: Tower Hill

Tower Bridge

2 Built in 1894, London's most famous bridge solved the problem of how to build a bridge for the city's east end that would also allow ships to enter the busiest port in the world. The answer lay in the bridge's lower span; its two halves can be raised, drawbridge-style, to let ships pass through. The pinnacled towers, which conceal the lifting mechanism, now house the **Tower Bridge Exhibition.** The high-level walkways between them provide breathtaking views of the river and some of London's best-known sites, including St. Paul's Cathedral and the London Eye to the west and Canary Wharf and Greenwich to the east. The bridge-opening system was electrified in 1974, but in the **Victorian engine room** below the South Tower, you

Despite having two towers of its own, Tower Bridge is named for the Tower of London.

can see the massive steam-powered pumps that drove the original lifting mechanism. In its early years, the bridge was raised more than 20 times a day. Now it is raised about three times a week to let through tall-masted sailing ships, naval vessels, and cruise ships.

Tower Bridge Rd., SE1 • www.towerbridge.org.uk • 020 7403 3761 • £££ • Closed Dec. 24–26 • Tube: Tower Hill or London Bridge

Whitechapel Gallery

3 Founded on the principle that art can inspire and lift the spirit, the Whitechapel opened in 1901. Since then, its program of temporary exhibitions has brought some of contemporary art's biggest names—including Pablo Picasso, Jackson Pollock, Mark Rothko, Frida Kahlo, and Lucien Freud, among others—to this traditionally deprived area of London. The recently expanded gallery also has a movie theater, a good art bookshop, a lively café, and an elegant restaurant.

77–82 Whitechapel High St., E1 • www.whitechapelgallery.org • 020 7522 7888 • Some temporary exhibitions £££ • Closed Mon. • Tube: Aldgate East

Brick Lane

4 East London's trendiest street is famous for its **curry houses,** cutting-edge arts scene, vintage clothing shops, and busy **Sunday market.** Wonderful aromas of spices and herbs emanate from the restaurants, and on Sundays street vendors sell a multitude of foods from around the world. Dazzling displays of graffiti cover the walls of several buildings. This is where underground artist Banksy made his name, and much of the current street art is equally dynamic. Vintage fashion has established itself as the style of East London, and clustered on and around Brick Lane are dozens of retro shops selling beautiful clothes. The music scene is also vibrant. Some of the city's most fashionable nightclubs, bars, and record stores are located in the neighborhood. Street signs here are in Bengali as well

EAST LONDON

Brick Lane's Sunday market buzzes with shoppers and diners.

as English, reflecting the ethnic origin of the local community. On the corner of Brick Lane and Fournier Street, look for the minaret of the community's **Jamme Masjid** (Great Mosque). Constructed as a Huguenot (French Protestant) chapel in 1743, the building has also served as a synagogue and a Methodist church, as successive waves of immigrants have settled in the district. It became a mosque in 1976. Brick Lane is at its liveliest on Sundays, when one of London's best flea markets takes over, and the local streets and warehouses fill up with stalls selling chic clothing, handmade crafts, culinary delights, antiques, art, music, and much more.

Shoreditch, E1 • www.visitbricklane.org • Tube: Aldgate East

Canary Wharf

⑤ On the Isle of Dogs—a former island bounded on three sides by a huge loop in the river—a group of gleaming skyscrapers rise from London's former docklands. The development, known as Canary Wharf, stands on the site of the 18th-century docks of the old West India Company, which supplied Britain with rum, sugar, chocolate, and other treats from the New World. The skycrapers house the world headquarters of many leading financial and media companies, while well-preserved warehouses brim with bars and restaurants, and office workers relax near small-craft moorings.

The **Museum of London Docklands,** housed in an old sugar warehouse (No. 1 Warehouse) on West India Quay, recounts London's history as a trading city from Roman times through to the 21st century. Three floors are packed with models, art, and documents illustrating the life and times of the communities that lived and worked along the river. In the Mudlarks interactive children's gallery, kids can weigh cargo or load a tea clipper.

Canary Wharf, E14 • Museum of London Docklands: West India Quay, E14; www.museumindocklands.org.uk; 020 7001 9844; closed Dec. 24–26 • Tube: Canary Wharf; DLR: West India Quay or Canary Wharf

Cutty Sark

6 You can spot the tip of the 152-foot (46.3 m) mast of this seafaring treasure above the surrounding buildings as you approach the dry dock where it rests on the south bank of the Thames. Launched in 1869, the *Cutty Sark* was one of the world's fastest ships. It began as a tea clipper, taking part in the annual race to carry that valued commodity from China to London. Next, it was retrofitted to carry wool and won the annual wool race from Melbourne, Australia, to London every year between 1885 and 1895. In 1954, the boat was brought to Greenwich and designated a memorial to the Merchant Navy. In 2007, a fire gutted it, but an extensive restoration project has returned the clipper to its former glory in readiness for its reopening to

GOOD **EATS**

■ **BELUGA CAFÉ**
Seafood features prominently on the menu. The terrace has fine views of the Canary Wharf skyline. **Unit 1, Port East Warehouse, E14, 020 7537 4665 ££££**

■ **MERAZ CAFÉ**
The restaurant serves a fusion of Indian, Bangladeshi, and Pakistani cooking known as Bharthian cuisine. **56 Hanbury St., E1, 020 7247 6999, £**

■ **TRAFALGAR TAVERN**
This popular pub beside the river was frequented by novelist Charles Dickens and Prime Minister William Gladstone. The restaurant serves modern British dishes. **6 Park Row, SE10, 020 8858 2909, ££££**

EAST LONDON

the public in 2012. The *Cutty Sark* stands beside the southern entrance to the Greenwich Foot Tunnel, which runs under the Thames to the Isle of Dogs on the north side of the river.

Greenwich Church St., SE10 • www.cuttysark.org.uk • 020 8858 2698 • DLR: Cutty Sark

Old Royal Naval College

7 One of architect Sir Christopher Wren's masterpieces, this pair of elegant colonnaded buildings graces the riverbank at Greenwich. Built by Queen Mary II between 1696 and 1712 for injured and retired sailors, the hospital was converted into a staff college for naval officers in 1873. Military cutbacks forced its closure in the 1990s. Many of the buildings are now part of Greenwich University, but two areas are open to the public. The spectacular **Painted Hall,** named for the huge wall and ceiling paintings by James Thornhill, was planned as the hospital's dining hall, but was considered too grand. It remained empty until January 1806, when Admiral Lord Nelson, hero of the Battle of Trafalgar against Napoleon's fleet, lay in state here. The **chapel,** rebuilt in neoclassical style in 1789 after a fire, is the work of architect James Stuart.

Greenwich, SE10 • www.oldroyalnavalcollege.org • 020 8269 4799 • Closed Dec. 24–26 • DLR: Cutty Sark

National Maritime Museum

8 A sound recording of breaking waves welcomes visitors to one of the world's largest maritime museums. Inside, ship models and plans, maps, navigational instruments, and trophies from all over the world recount Britain's history on the high seas. Look closely at Nelson's jacket, and you can see the hole made by the French musket ball that killed him at the Battle of Trafalgar in October, 1805. Admire the wine set a grateful Charles Dickens presented to the captain of the steamship *Britannia* after a particularly stormy transatlantic voyage in 1842. Kids can enjoy the **All Hands Gallery,** and everyone can try their hand at steering a modern ship in the professional **bridge simulator.** The museum's extensive collection of maritime art, including J. M. W. Turner's oil painting of the Battle of Trafalgar, is on show in the nearby **Queen's House.**

Romney Rd., SE10 • www.nmm.ac.uk • 020 8858 4422• Closed Dec. 24–26
• DLR: Cutty Sark

Royal Observatory

9 Perched on the hill behind the National Maritime Museum, the Royal Observatory was founded in 1675 by King Charles II for research in navigation. On display are some of the world's first portable timepieces, which were used for navigation at sea. The most popular feature, located in the courtyard, is the **prime meridian**—0° longitude—which divides the world into East and West. At night, the Observatory projects a laser light into the sky along the meridian. The site also includes a **planetarium.**

Blackheath Ave., SE10 • www.nmm.ac.uk • 020 8858 4422 • £££ • Closed Dec. 24–26 • DLR: Cutty Sark

EAST LONDON

Stand astride the prime meridian with a foot in each hemisphere at the Royal Observatory.

Tower of London

Fortress, royal residence, prison, and home to the Crown Jewels, the medieval Tower has a long and at times bloody history.

The Tower's round turret, second from right, contained the first royal observatory.

William the Conqueror ordered the construction of the Tower in the 11th century as a fortress. Successive kings altered and expanded it throughout the 12th and 13th centuries. During its 900-year history, it has been used as a royal home, an arsenal, a mint, and a menagerie—but it is probably most famous as a prison. Of the many "guests" kept here—including kings, queens, advisors, and former royal favorites—some were executed on Tower Green. The Yeoman Warders, or Beefeaters, act as guards and guides.

■ ROYAL ARMOR

The central stronghold, known as the **White Tower,** is the oldest part of the fortress. It houses an exhibition of royal armor, including a large decorative suit made for King Henry VIII in 1540 and a suit covered in gold leaf made in 1612 that belonged to King Charles I.

■ CROWN JEWELS

Among the dazzling array of 23,578 jewels on display in the **Jewel House** is **St. Edward's Crown,** decorated with sapphires, tourmalines, amethysts, topazes, and citrines, and last worn by Queen Elizabeth II at her coronation in 1953. The crown weighs an uncomfortable 4.9 pounds (2.22 kg), and many monarchs have declined to wear it, opting instead for the **Imperial State Crown,** which is decorated with 2,868 diamonds, 273 pearls, 17 sapphires, 11 emeralds, and five rubies.

■ FEATHERED GUARDIANS

Tower Green is the place to see the **ravens** that guard the tower. According to legend, if they ever left the Tower, the White Tower would collapse and disaster would engulf England. To ensure this never happened, King

Charles II decreed that there must always be six ravens in residence.

■ TRAITORS' GATE

In the 13th century, King Edward I built a gate at river level beneath **St. Thomas's Tower** to provide access to the Tower by boat. In Tudor times, prisoners of the monarch—many of whom were accused of treason—arrived this way.

■ PRINCES IN THE TOWER

The **Bloody Tower** acquired its name in the 16th century because it was thought this was where Richard of Gloucester (later King Richard III) murdered his two nephews, Edward V and his brother Richard, in 1483. Two hundred years later, the skeletons of two boys were discovered here. A room houses an exhibition about their disappearance. Others imprisoned in the tower included Sir Walter Raleigh, a favorite of Queen Elizabeth I. A room is furnished as it might have been when he was here.

Tower of London, Tower Hill, EC3 • www.hrp.org.uk/toweroflondon • 0844 482 7777 • £££££
• Closed Jan. 1 and Dec. 24–26 • Tube: Tower Hill

Maritime City

For more than 200 years, London was at the heart of the world's most powerful maritime power. The Royal Navy enforced British rule across much of the globe, and British trading ships imported large quantities of tea, sugar, spices, tobacco, and a host of other commodities. By the 19th century, new warehouses, docks, and shipbuilders had transformed East London into the world's busiest port.

St. Katharine Docks (above) by Tower Bridge have been converted into a marina; in the early 20th century, the area around Tower Bridge (right) was a working port.

Roman Port

The Romans chose the stretch of riverbank between Tower Bridge and London Bridge for their new capital. The river here flowed wide and deep enough to take seagoing vessels, yet was narrow enough for the construction of a bridge—prerequisites for a successful inland port.

The World's Warehouse

Beginning in the 17th century, Britain's empire grew based on global trade, and the port of London expanded into the biggest ever known. By the 18th century, wharves and warehouses, with moorings for hundreds of ships, lined both banks, while a continuous parade of tall-masted ships thronged the river.

It was a chaotic, dangerous place. Crews from all corners of the world waited for their ships to be unloaded, and gangs of thieves prowled at night. Thousands of dockworkers were employed loading and unloading cargo, yet the port still could not meet the expanding demand from larger and more numerous ships. A solution was found in the early 19th century with the creation of the West India, East India, and Surrey Commercial Docks, among others. These walled, wet docks provided safe berths, efficient unloading, and better links to the industries of East London.

Decline & Rebirth

During World War II, more than 25,000 bombs fell on or around the docks. Some basins were repaired, others were filled in, and trade continued. Then, in the 1960s, the new container ships proved too large for the port's facilities and went elsewhere. Within 20 years, all the docks had closed. A huge revitalization program has seen the Docklands area emerge as a flourishing financial center, and soaring waterfront offices and glossy apartment buildings have created a new riverscape.

FLOATING **MUSEUM**

The most visible sign of the Royal Navy in London today is the cruiser **H.M.S. Belfast** (*Morgan's Lane, SE1, http:// hmsbelfast.iwm.org.uk, ££££, closed Dec. 24–26*). The ship is one of the most powerful ever built for the Royal Navy. It saw service in World War II and Korea and was used for peacekeeping duties in the 1950s and '60s. Now it is moored on the Thames close to Tower Bridge and offers visitors a taste of life aboard a 20th-century warship.

Hip East London Shops

East London has some of Europe's hippest alternative shopping. While the city's West End has contemporary designers, the east has developed a taste for stylish clothes from yesteryear. In the boutiques around Brick Lane, you can pick up a classic 1940s dress for a fraction of the cost of a new design.

■ BEYOND RETRO

With vintage clothes such as 1960s blazers, 1940s dresses, and 1980s pantsuits, Beyond Retro prides itself on finding the best 20th-century fashion. With a wide range of clothing on offer, you should be able to find something that appeals to you, and with prices at around £30 ($48) for a dress, a purchase won't break the bank.

110–112 Cheshire St., E2 • www.beyondretro
.com • 020 7729 9001 • Closed Dec. 25–26
• Tube: Liverpool Street

■ VINTAGE BASEMENT

Unique items from the 1950s through the 1980s fill the racks of this shop. It's fun to browse through the vintage clothing—and if you do make a purchase, you're unlikely to see anyone else wearing the same outfit.

7 Cheshire St., E2 • www.vintagebasement.co.uk
• 020 7729 2908 • Closed Dec. 25
• Tube: Liverpool Street

■ SUNDAY UPMARKET

Every Sunday, more than 140 stalls selling unique clothes, bags, jewelry, home accessories, and more fill this former brewery. The majority of goods on sale are handcrafted, one-off items produced by the stallholders themselves. In the lively food section, independent caterers from around the world cook up cherished family recipes. Their stalls alone make the visit worthwhile.

The Old Truman Brewery, Brick Lane, E1
• www.sundayupmarket.co.uk • 020 7770 6028
• Open Sun. • Tube: Liverpool Street

■ ROUGH TRADE EAST

Since opening in 2007, Rough Trade East has become London's most popular music shop. The store regularly hosts concerts, including some given by the world's top bands, such as Radiohead and Blur. If you are lucky, you might see a free show.

Rough Trade has a "snug" area with sofas and tables where music fans congregate.

Whether you are looking for the rarest bands or the hottest new thing, the staff members are experts in all things musical and more than happy to help.

91 Brick Lane, E1 • www.roughtrade.com • 020 7392 7790 • Closed Dec. 25 • Tube: Liverpool Street

■ APPLETREE BOUTIQUE

From its humble beginnings as a market stall, the Appletree Boutique has become one of the most fashionable ladies' clothing shops in London, selling contemporary printed dresses and accessories. The stock changes regularly.

104 Commercial St., E1 • www.appletree boutique.co.uk • 020 7377 5900 • Closed Jan. 1, Dec. 24–25 • Tube: Liverpool Street

■ INTERIOR ADDICT

Interior Addict has just opened its very first London showroom, offering affordable but exciting contemporary furniture and reproductions of classic designs.

50-52 Commercial St., E1 • www.interior addict.com • 020 7377 1855 • Closed Dec. 25 • Tube: Liverpool Street

PART 3

Travel Essentials

PLANNING YOUR TRIP

When to Go

January, February, and **March** are good months for getting into popular plays and operas, and enjoying museums without the long lines. For sports, there are plenty of soccer and rugby matches, and the Oxford vs. Cambridge boat race takes place on the Thames. Daffodils carpet the lawns of the parks, while trees burst into leaf.

April and **May** mark an increase in events, such as arts festivals, houses that open only for the summer months, the culmination of the soccer season, the start of the cricket season, and the popular Chelsea Flower Show.

June brings the summer-long season of open-air concerts at Kenwood House and Marble Hill House and the All England Lawn Tennis Championships at Wimbledon. Ceremonial events peak, too, with Beating Retreat and Trooping the Colour.

July and **August** are when museums and theaters fill up with visitors. Cultural highlights include the nightly Henry Wood Promenade ("The Proms") concerts at the Royal Albert Hall. Cricket continues through the summer, and, in 2012, London will transform into a sporting heaven when the Olympic Games will hold events throughout the city.

September and **October** mix festivals on the Thames and in Covent Garden with major art shows, operas, and plays. In the parks, sunny days bring the crowds, especially on weekends and public holidays.

November and **December** are strong on festivities: Shops and streets are decorated for the holidays, theater tickets need to be reserved in advance, and an abundance of music is performed in concert halls, cathedrals, and churches.

Climate

British weather can be a daily surprise, and a sunny morning can become a wet afternoon. Be prepared and carry a fold-up umbrella and consider waterproof shoes.

Passports & Visas

Nationals of the United States, Canada, Australia, and New Zealand can enter the United Kingdom with just a passport.

HOW TO GET TO CENTRAL LONDON

From the Airports

Gatwick (*www.gatwick airport.com, 08443 351 802*) lies 30 miles (48 km) south of central London. The Gatwick Express (*www.gatwickexpress .com, 08458 501 530*) train runs to Victoria, a 35-minute ride, every 15 minutes by day and less frequently by night. By road, the Easybus (*www.easybus.co.uk*) takes around 70 minutes and departs about every 20 minutes, 24 hours a day. Taking a taxi costs more than £60 ($100).

Heathrow (*www.heathrow airport.com, 08443 351 801*) is the city's main airport, 15 miles (24 km) west of central London. By rail, the Heathrow Express (*www.heathrowexpress .com, 08456 001 515*) to Paddington, a 20-minute ride, runs every 15 minutes between 5:07 a.m. and 11:42 p.m. By Tube, the Piccadilly line, a 40- to 60-minute ride, runs regularly from 5:02 a.m. to 12:00 a.m. through central London. National Express (*www.nationalexpress.com, 08717 818 181*) buses go to Victoria Coach Station every 30 minutes and take 60 to 90 minutes. Taking a taxi costs around £50 ($82).

London City Airport (*www.londoncityairport.com, 020 7646 0000*) is a small airport 9 miles (14 km) east of central London. It has a Docklands Light Railway station with links to Canary Wharf and Bank, both on the Tube and DLR.

Stansted (*www.stansted airport.com, 08443 351 803*) is 35 miles (56 km) northeast of central London; travel by rail is faster than road. Stansted Express (*www.stanstedexpress .com*) to Liverpool Street station takes 42 minutes and runs every 15 minutes between 6 a.m. and 11:59 p.m. (1:30 a.m. Sat. and Sun.).

By Train or Bus

Eurostar trains (*www.euro star.com, 020 7646 0088*) arrive at St. Pancras International (*www.stpancras.com, 020 7843 7688*) from Paris, Disneyland Paris, Brussels, and Lille.

National trains (*www.national rail.co.uk, 08457 484 950*) service Charing Cross, Euston, King's Cross, Liverpool Street, Paddington, St. Pancras, Victoria, and Waterloo stations.

Long-distance bus services arrive at Victoria Coach Station. National Express (*www.national express.com, 08717 818 181*) is Britain's biggest bus company, while Eurolines (*www.euro lines.co.uk, 01582 404 511*) travels to the Continent.

GETTING AROUND

London Transportation

Taxis, although fun, are just one transportation experience, and the costs mount up very quickly. Take the Tube or a bus, and if you are lost, just ask for directions. Transport for London (*www.tfl.gov.uk, 08432 221 234*) runs an excellent journey planner on its website, offering the quickest and easiest way to complete your journey.

Taxi

There are two kinds of taxis: the "black cab" and the minicab. Black cab drivers have all passed "The Knowledge" exams and know the city extremely well. To use one, either go to a taxi stand, call a company such as Radio Taxis (*www.radiotaxis.co.uk, 020 7272 0272*), or hail one on the street. Minicabs may have uninsured cars and unprofessional drivers.

Mass Transit

Underground fares are structured according to nine zones, while buses charge per journey. Tickets can be bought for each individual trip, or you can buy a Travelcard, but the most economical way is an Oyster card. These can be bought at any Tube/DLR station for a deposit of £3 ($4.90). Load money onto the card at the ticket office or touchscreen machines, and touch the card on the yellow disks at ticket barriers at the start and the conclusion of your journey. For buses, only touch on entry. Oyster card fares are less than other fares.

Bus

There is nothing quite like rumbling through London on a bus, looking at the people, buildings, advertisements, and street art. All bus stops have maps showing bus routes and nearby stops. Pay with an Oyster card or Travelcard, or a ticket bought in advance.

Tube (Underground)

This huge system of a dozen lines and 270 stations snakes all over London and carries 2.5 million people a day. London's Tube (subway) is well lit, easy to use, and safe. First, plot your route on the Tube map. Then, buy a Travelcard, Oyster card, or individual ticket. Use this to pass through the automatic barriers, get on the correct color-coded line, and ensure you are traveling in the right direction. To change lines, follow the signs to the connecting line on the platform. Use your ticket or card to exit through the barriers. When in doubt, ask; Londoners get lost too.

Bike

New additions to London's transportation scene are easy-to-rent bikes. Pay £1 ($1.65) for 24-hour access to release-codes for the many bike stands dotted around the city, either at the stand, online (*www.tfl.gov.uk*), or by phone (*08450 263 630*). Journeys under 30 minutes are free, and for more than 30 minutes, costs £1. When you're finished, lock the bike back into its stand.

Docklands Light Railway (DLR)

This high-level railway (*www.tfl.gov.uk, 08432 221 234*) runs from Bank and Tower Gateway stations, and on through Docklands and East London.

Organized Sightseeing

Even the most independent traveler may wish to take a tour sometimes. Bus tours give an overview of the city, walking tours open your eyes to a street's history, river tours provide a new perspective, and some tours get you into places usually closed to the public.

TRAVEL **ESSENTIALS**

Bus Tours
Big Bus Company (www.bigbus tours.com, 020 7233 9533);
Original London Sightseeing Tour (www.theoriginaltour.com, 020 8877 1722).

River Tours
The best website for boat tours is www.tfl.gov.uk.

Specialist Tours
Companies such as **City Discovery** (www.city-discovery.com) offer specialist, in-depth tours of Westminster Abbey, St. Paul's Cathedral, and other attractions.

Tailor-made Tours
For a guide with the highest qualifications, the Blue Badge, contact **Tour Guides** (www.tour guides.co.uk, 020 7495 5504).

Walking Tours
Citisights (www.chr.org.uk, 020 8806 3742); **Original London Walks** (www.walks.com, 020 7624 3978) has a huge variety of walks led by enthusiasts.

PRACTICAL ADVICE

Electricity
The supply is 230V, with a permitted range of 216.2–253V, and 50 cycles per second (kHz). Plugs are three-pin. U.S. appliances need a voltage transformer and an adapter.

Money Matters
Sterling currency is used throughout Britain: 100 pence make 1 pound. Coins are in denominations of 1p, 2p, 5p, 10p, 20p, 50p, £1, and £2. Notes are in £5, £10, £20, and £50.

What's Going On?
Time Out (www.timeout.com), published on Tuesdays, provides exhaustive lists of London activities, together with reliable reviews and previews. Quality newspapers include the *Daily Telegraph,* the *Financial Times,* and the *Guardian;* London's only evening paper is the free *Evening Standard,* daily Monday to Friday. The *Metro* is a free morning tabloid, widely available at Tube stations.

Opening Hours
Shops are open seven days a week, but many limit opening hours on Sundays. Late night shopping takes place on Wednesday (Knightsbridge) and Thursday (Oxford St., Regent St., and Covent Garden). Banks open Monday to Friday from 9:30 a.m. to 5 p.m. Chequepoint branches at 550 Oxford Street and 71 Gloucester Road open late.

Post Offices
Stamps can be bought at post offices and some newsstands and shops; Trafalgar Square Post Office, on William IV Street, stays open late. Mailboxes are red.

Public Holidays
January 1, Good Friday, Easter Monday, first Monday in May, last Monday in May, last Monday in August, December 25 and 26. If you're traveling across the country on any of these days, expect delays.

Restrooms
Otherwise known as toilets, lavatories, loos, WCs, ladies, and gents. If the public restrooms are unsavory, slip into the nearest large department store or hotel.

Smoking
Smoking is prohibited in all bars, pubs, restaurants, and other enclosed public places.

Telephones
The city code for London is 020. (When calling from the U.S., omit the initial "0.") To make a call within London, either use coins or buy a BT phone card from a newsstand or other shop. Omit the 020 city code and dial the eight-digit number. Outside London, numbers usually have a three- or five-digit code and a six-figure number. Evenly spaced beeps mean the number is busy; a solid sound means the number is unobtainable.

The London Pass
This is a bargain way of visiting several of London's fee-paying attractions (www.londonpass.com, 08702 429 988).

Time Differences
GMT (Greenwich mean time) is standard time; BST (British Summer Time) is one hour ahead of GMT and runs from late March to late October. GMT is five hours ahead of U.S. Eastern Standard Time.

Tourist Information
VisitBritain Offices:

In the United States:
Los Angeles *1766 Wilshire Blvd., Suite 1200, 310/481-2989.*
New York *551 Fifth Ave., Suite 701, 800/462-2748*

In Canada:
Toronto *160 Bloor St. East, 416/646-6674*

Useful Websites
www.a-zmaps.co.uk
www.bbc.co.uk/london
For news, travel, weather, entertainment, and sports
www.culture24.org.uk
Includes most London museum information
www.londonnet.co.uk
Restaurants, bars, and nightlife
www.londontown.com
Basic information on top sights, hotels, etc.
www.officiallondontheatre .co.uk
On-the-day information on half-price theater tickets
www.riverthames.co.uk
Places and events on the river
www.streetmap.co.uk
Plan your day, then print out the street plan
www.tfl.gov.uk
For all transport
www.ticketmaster.co.uk
For tickets to events
www.timeout.com
For all event listings
www.trailfinders.com
For all travel booking
www.visitbritain.com
The British Tourist Board
www.visitlondon.com
The London Tourist Board

Visitors with Disabilities
Facilities are generally good for visitors with disabilities. Artsline *(54 Charlton St., NW1, www .artsline.org.uk)* has advice on access to entertainment and arts venues. RADAR (the Royal Society for Disability and Rehabilitation) provides information on tour operators that cater specifically to disabled travelers *(www.radar .org.uk, 020 7250 3222).*

EMERGENCIES

Police, Fire, & Ambulance
To summon any of these services, dial 999 from any telephone, free of charge.

Lost Property
Always inform the police to validate insurance claims. Report a lost passport to your embassy. For lost property on the Tube, buses, black taxi cabs, and London Overground, contact Transport for London Lost Property Office *(200 Baker St., NW1, www.tfl.gov.uk, 020 7918 2000, Mon.–Fri. 8:30 a.m.– 4 p.m.).* Property lost on the DLR is held for 48 hours at Poplar Station *(020 7363 9550)* and then forwarded to the office at 200 Baker St. (above).

Health Precautions
If you need a doctor or dentist, ask your hotel reception for advice. If the problem is minor, go to the nearest chemist (pharmacy) and speak to the pharmacist. For insurance claims, keep receipts for all treatments and medicines.

National Health Service (N.H.S.) Hospitals
Hospitals with 24-hour emergency departments include:
Chelsea and Westminster Hospital *(369 Fulham Rd., SW10, 020 8746 8000)*
University College Hospital *(Gower St., entrance in Grafton Way, WC1, 08451 555 000).*

Other Facilities
For an optician and on-site repair workshop, try **Aitchison** *(127a Sloane St., SW1, 020 7730 4870).* Those with more serious eye problems should seek help at **Moorfields Eye Hospital** *(City Rd., EC1, 020 7253 3411).*

Chemists (Pharmacies)
Many drugs freely available in the U.S. cannot be bought over the counter in the UK. Be sure to bring sufficient supplies of medicines from home. If more are needed, take the wrapping with a full printed description of its contents to the chemist for advice on purchasing the nearest equivalent. Chemists that open from 9 a.m. until midnight include **Bliss Chemist** *(5 Marble Arch, W1, 020 7723 6116).*

Embassies & Consulates
Canadian High Commission, *1 Grosvenor Sq., W1, www.canadainternational.gc.ca, 020 7258 6600*
Embassy of the United States of America, *Grosvenor Sq., W1, http://london.usembassy.gov, 020 7499 9000*

HOTELS

Location is the key to a successful London visit. There are hotels of every level of luxury, from simple to exotic, but their location is paramount: London is very big; hours—and money—can be wasted moving around. You must also be aware of your budget. Sleeping in London is expensive—the average room in London costs around $150 a night, but the high-end hotels can charge many times more. It is wise to figure out where you will be spending your days and evenings, then choose a well-placed hotel that suits your lifestyle, plans, and budget. And be sure to plan ahead—London has plenty of hotel rooms, but the best get booked up in advance.

London's hotels have undergone a revolution, especially at the top end. The emphasis is on design-led hotels, such as Kit Kemp's Firmdale hotels, including the Soho with its fashionable bar. Myhotel, which opened in Chelsea in late 1998, was Terence Conran's first hotel, planned with a feng shui expert as an "oasis of calm." Subsequently, he lavishly transformed the Great Eastern Hotel (now the Andaz) in the City. Ian Schrager and Philipe Starck have brought New York panache and success to London with new hotels, including the Sanderson and St. Martin's Lane.

Boutique hotels have long been established in South Kensington with such successes as The Gore. Now up-market choices has spread right across central London—to Hazlitt's in Soho, Charlotte Street in Fitzrovia, the Rookery in Clerkenwell, and Threadneedles in the heart of the City.

More traditional luxury hotels, such as the Ritz, Savoy, Berkeley, Claridge's, and Dorchester, are now joined by the Mandarin Oriental group's totally overhauled Hyde Park Hotel. Other refurbished hotels include Le Méridien Piccadilly and the St. Pancras Renaissance. Indeed, lavish refurbishments abound at all levels, while newly built hotels spanning all price brackets open monthly.

It is important to make reservations well in advance. And try to save money by asking about special deals when making a reservation. These may include weekends or during the quiet month of February, when you may find a better deal at a deluxe hotel than at a popular business hotel. New hotels often offer discounts while they deal with teething troubles. Some hotels have economic family rooms; others, such as the Citadines London Trafalgar Square, have a kitchen in each room.

When reserving, you may be asked for a deposit or for your credit card number. Check the room rate carefully: It should include the 20 percent VAT tax, but occasionally prices are given without this.

If anything goes wrong during your stay, talk to the duty manager. If the problem isn't resolved, talk to the manager, then put it in writing.

Visit London has a hotel information and reservation section on its website (*www.visitlondon.com*) and publishes the reliable booklet "Where to Stay & What to Do." It also handles serious complaints.

Some of the nicest hotels are in old buildings that may not have all the modern conveniences. If you have particular needs in comfort, services, or anything else, check that your hotel can provide them before you book.

Visitors with disabilities can obtain information on suitable places to stay from **Tourism for All** (*c/o Vitalise, Shap Rd., Kendal, Cumbria LA9 6NZ, www.tourismforall.org.uk, 08451 249 971, or 0044 1539 814 683 for calls from outside the UK*).

Apartments
Those visiting for longer periods may wish to rent a serviced apartment on a weekly basis. Rates can be very competitive even in the city center. Agencies specializing in vacation rentals include **Coach House Rentals** (*www.chsrentals.com, 020 8772 1939*). **The Kings Wardrobe** (*www.bridgestreet.co.uk, 020 7792*

2222) has modest, well-priced apartments near St. Paul's Cathedral. **No. 5 Maddox Street** *(www.living-rooms .co.uk, 020 7647 0200)* has suites equipped with workstations, balconies, and minimalist decor. **Citadines London Trafalgar Square** *(www.citadines.com, 0800 376 3898)* has 189 simple studios and one- and two-bedroom apartments in an unbeatable location. Citadines also has properties in Barbican, Holborn, and South Kensington.

Organization
Hotels listed here have been grouped first according to neighborhood, then listed alphabetically by price range.

Price Range
An indication of the cost of a double room in the high season is given by £ signs.

£££££	Over £275
££££	£201–£275
£££	£151–£200
££	£75–£150
£	Under £75

Text Symbols
🛈 *No. of Guest Rooms*
🚇 *Tube*

THE CITY
London's historic heart has some hotels whose elegance matches their history.

■ Andaz
£££££
40 LIVERPOOL STREET EC2
TEL 020 7961 1234
FAX 020 7961 1235
**www.london.liverpoolstreet
.andaz.hyatt.com**
Conran took a grand Victorian railway station and stylishly transformed it into a modern City hotel, though now renamed and run by Hyatt.
🛈 *267* 🚇 *Liverpool Street*

■ Threadneedles
£££££
5 THREADNEEDLE STREET EC2
TEL 020 7657 8080
FAX 020 7657 8100
www.theetoncollection.com
The City's original boutique hotel is inside a fine former Midland Bank building. The rooms are equipped with plasma TVs and other gadgets.
🛈 *69* 🚇 *Bank*

■ Rookery
££££
12 PETER'S LANE, COWCROSS STREET EC1
TEL 020 7336 0931
FAX 020 7336 0932
www.rookeryhotel.com
Simple but tasteful rooms in Georgian row houses are under the same management as the successful Hazlitt's (see p. 183).
🛈 *33* 🚇 *Farringdon*

WESTMINSTER
At the heart of London, close to many key sights,

the capital's grandest hotels have exceptional restaurants and lively bars, which make excellent rendezvous spots.

■ The Athenaeum
£££££
116 PICCADILLY W1
TEL 020 7499 3464
FAX 020 7493 1860
www.athenaeumhotel.com
The elegant comfort and high level of service draw guests back to the Athenaeum's rooms and apartments, as do Windsor Lounge teas and the spa. Higher rooms have park views.
🛈 *156* 🚇 *Hyde Park Corner*

■ Brown's
£££££
ALBEMARLE STREET W1
TEL 020 7493 6020
FAX 020 7493 9381
www.brownshotel.com
Traditional English elegance in the heart of old Mayfair, it has been totally refurbished. Roaring fires and creaking floorboards are an echo of Mayfair mansions. Especially good traditional tea.
🛈 *117* 🚇 *Green Park*

■ Claridge's
£££££
BROOK STREET W1
TEL 020 7629 8860
FAX 020 7499 2210
www.claridges.co.uk
The queen's state guests move here after Buckingham Palace. Huge corner suites. Glorious public rooms include the grand dining room, design by Thierry Despont and Diane von Furstenberg, food by Gordon Ramsay.
🛈 *203* 🚇 *Bond Street*

HOTELS

■ **The Connaught**
£££££
CARLOS PLACE W1
TEL 020 7499 7070
FAX 020 7495 3262
www.the-connaught.co.uk
In this most discreet of
London hotels the famous can
remain anonymous. Recently
refurbished, it boasts Michelin-
starred food from Hélène
Darroze and two fine bars,
the Coburg and Connaught.
🛈 122 🚇 Bond Street

■ **The Dorchester**
£££££
PARK LANE W1
TEL 020 7629 8888
FAX 020 7409 0114
www.thedorchester.com
Lavishly redone, including the
rooftop Oliver Messel rooms
and a luscious spa. Guests
and visitors can enjoy fine
Promenade teas, the zippy bar,
and restaurants: the traditional
Grill, three-Michelin-star Alain
Ducasse, and opulent China
Tang (Cantonese).
🛈 250 🚇 Hyde Park Corner

■ **Four Seasons**
£££££
HAMILTON PLACE
PARK LANE W1
TEL 020 7499 0888
FAX 020 7493 1895
www.fourseasons.com/london
Refurbished in 2010, an
intelligently designed hotel
with excellent rooms and
suites; some of London's top
chefs have worked in the Four
Seasons restaurant (modern
European). A second hotel is
at Canary Wharf (see p. 187).
🛈 192 🚇 Hyde Park Corner

■ **Landmark Hotel**
£££££
222 MARYLEBONE ROAD NW1
TEL 020 7631 8000
FAX 020 7631 8080
www.landmarklondon.co.uk
The spectacular Winter
Garden, a palm court that
operates all day, sets the
tone for this converted grand
late-Victorian building. Large
rooms with good bathrooms.
Surprisingly well-located.
🛈 300 🚇 Marylebone

■ **Le Méridien
Piccadilly**
£££££
21 PICCADILLY W1
TEL 020 7734 8000
FAX 020 7437 3574
www.lemeridienpiccadilly
.co.uk
Located at the crossroads of
St. James's, Mayfair, and
theaterland. Guests enjoy fine
rooms, a splendid health club
and spa, stylish afternoon
tea in the Oak Room, and
excellent bars.
🛈 266 🚇 Piccadilly Circus

■ **Metropolitan**
£££££
19 OLD PARK LANE W1
TEL 020 7447 1000
www.metropolitan.como.bz
The Metropolitan has a
reputation for cutting-edge
design and matching guests,
checking into its rooms
and apartments. Getting
a reservation at its Nobu
restaurant (Japanese) is hard,
though the once exclusive
Met Bar is less trendy than it
was in the past.
🛈 150 🚇 Hyde Park Corner

■ **The Ritz**
£££££
150 PICCADILLY W1
TEL 020 7493 8181
FAX 020 7493 2687
www.theritzlondon.com
Exquisite hotel overlooking
Green Park, whose painted-
and-gilded dining room is
London's most beautiful. Tea is
disappointing, but the bar is a
promenade for the stylish. Note
the formal dress code: no jeans
or sneakers, and men must
wear jacket and tie.
🛈 136 🚇 Green Park

■ **The Stafford**
£££££
16–18 ST. JAMES'S PLACE SW1
TEL 020 7493 0111
FAX 020 7493 7121
www.kempinski.com
One of London's most
luxurious small hotels, tucked
down an alley off St. James's
Street. There is a delightful
dining room and fine wines
stored in 350-year-old cellars.
🛈 105 🚇 Green Park

■ **The Trafalgar Hotel**
£££££
2 SPRING GARDENS W1
TEL 020 7870 2900
FAX 020 7870 2911
www.thetrafalgar.com
Designed to attract younger
guests, this lifestyle hotel
has sharp service, good design,
and the popular Rockwell Bar
and roof bar.
🛈 129 🚇 Charing Cross

■ **Durrants Hotel**
££££
26–32 GEORGE STREET W1
TEL 020 7935 8131
www.durrantshotel.co.uk

The hotel opened when its Georgian terrace was quite new, in 1790, and descendants of that family maintain its comfortable tone today.

(i) 92　**(train)** *Bond Street*

SOUTH BANK

The strip along the south bank of the Thames is one of the city's most exciting and innovative areas.

■ London Marriott County Hall
££££££

COUNTY HALL, WESTMINSTER BRIDGE ROAD SE1
TEL 020 7928 5200
FAX 020 7928 5300
www.marriott.co.uk

This hotel is in part of the old London County Hall building. Some rooms have river views, and the leisure facilities, including a pool, are first class.

(i) 200　**(train)** *Westminster/Waterloo*

■ London Bridge Hotel
££££

8–18 LONDON BRIDGE STREET SE1
TEL 020 7855 2200
www.london-bridge-hotel .co.uk

This well-equipped and modern hotel is just south of London Bridge, a short walk from the popular Borough market and the City's pubs and restaurants. There are no river views.

(i) 138　**(train)** *London Bridge*

■ Mad Hatter
££

3–7 STAMFORD STREET SE1
TEL 020 7401 9222
www.fullershotels.com

A welcome new arrival located behind South Bank theaters, near Blackfriars Bridge, a short walk to the City or taxi to the West End. No river views.

(i) 30　**(train)** *Blackfriars*

■ Premier Inn
££

COUNTY HALL, BELVEDERE ROAD SE1
TEL 0871 5278648
www.premierinn.com

This no-frills, good value hotel behind the deluxe London Marriott has an excellent location. No river views.

(i) 313　**(train)** *Westminster/Waterloo*

TRAFALGAR SQUARE & SOHO

The heart of the city, Trafalgar Square is close to many of London's major attractions, many of its theaters, and Soho's vibrant nightlife.

■ St. Martin's Lane
£££££

45 ST. MARTIN'S LANE WC2
TEL 020 7300 5500
www.stmartinslane.com

Hovering between West End theaters and Covent Garden restaurants, Philippe Starck's dramatically minimalist rooms and extensive bars attract design-conscious clients.

(i) 204　**(train)** *Covent Garden/Leicester Square*

■ The Soho Hotel
£££££

4 RICHMOND MEWS DEAN STREET W1
TEL 020 7559 3000
www.firmdale.com

Designer Kit Kemp's sixth London hotel (see *www .firmdale.com* for the others) mixes country style with urban simplicity in a bare brick building. Lovely bathrooms and a buzzing bar and restaurant.

(i) 91　**(train)** *Tottenham Court Road*

■ Dean Street Townhouse
££££

71 DEAN STREET W1
TEL 020 7434 1775
www.deanstreettown house.com

This chic Soho hotel opened in 2010 in a converted four-story Georgian house with a rich history. Public spaces are opulent, while the rooms have original features and a decorative palette of mostly soft browns and off-whites. The popular dining room (open to non-patrons) has a traditional, clublike look and atmosphere, and serves classic British food at breakfast, lunch, tea, and dinner.

(i) 39　**(train)** *Tottenham Court Road*

■ Hazlitt's
££££

6 FRITH STREET W1
TEL 020 7434 1771
FAX 020 7439 1524
www.hazlittshotel.com

Once the home of writer William Hazlitt (1778–1830), this gracious building is now a town-house hotel in the heart of Soho. There are antiques in the beautifully furnished rooms. Ideal for theater and museum visits. As this is a landmark hotel, there are no elevators. There is minimal room service.

(i) 30　**(train)** *Tottenham Court Road*

HOTELS

■ Sanctum Soho Hotel
££££
20 WARWICK STREET W1
TEL 020 7292 6100
www.sanctumsoho.com
This modern, minimalistic hotel, has a great location close to Regent Street and a rooftop garden terrace and bar.
ⓘ 30 🚇 Piccadilly Circus

COVENT GARDEN TO LUDGATE HILL
Hotels range from grand to bargain in this superb location in the heart of London.

■ One Aldwych
£££££
1 ALDWYCH WC2
TEL 020 7300 1000
FAX 020 7300 1001
www.campbellgray hotels.com
One of London's most dynamic contemporary renovations. Built in 1907 for the long-since gone *Morning Post* newspaper, One Aldwych has been transformed by Gordon Campbell-Gray and Mary Fox Linton into a state-of-the-art hotel. There is serious art on the walls, and a sumptuous and extensive health spa. Indigo restaurant and formal adjoining Axis restaurant.
ⓘ 105 🚇 Charing Cross

■ The Savoy
£££££
STRAND WC2
TEL 020 7836 4343
FAX 020 7240 2398
www.fairmont.com/savoy
One of London's most famous hotels is in an ideal stylish location for mixing City with West End. It reopened in 2010, after a major refurbishment. The American Bar, Pavilion Room teas, and River Room restaurant are all top-notch.
ⓘ 268 🚇 Charing Cross

■ Covent Garden
££££
10 MONMOUTH STREET WC2
TEL 020 7806 1000
FAX 020 7806 1100
www.firmdale.com
The wood-paneled drawing room and atmospheric Tiffany library, together with the individualized, brightly colored rooms, make this hotel seem far from urban London's hub.
ⓘ 58 🚇 Covent Garden

■ Crowne Plaza London—The City
££££
19 NEW BRIDGE STREET, EC4
TEL 0871 9429198
FAX 020 7438 8088
www.ichotelsgroup.com
Superbly located between Ludgate Hill and Fleet Street, and with a vibrant bar and the excellent Refettorio restaurant, this hotel is ideal for mixing business with pleasure.
ⓘ 203 🚇 Blackfriars

■ Haymarket Hotel
££££
1 SUFFOLK PLACE SW1
TEL 020 7470 4000
www.firmdale.com
One of the Firmdale group's stable of excellent, intimate hotels, with an ideal location— the Haymarket is at the heart of the theater district. Rooms are calm, quiet, and comfortable, and facilities include a gym and swimming pool. The hotel also offers beauty treatments.
ⓘ 50 🚇 Piccadilly Circus/ Leicester Square

■ The Fielding Hotel
££
4 BROAD COURT, BOW STREET WC2
TEL 020 7836 8305
FAX 020 7497 0064
www.thefieldinghotel.co.uk
Quiet, simple accommodation in a pedestrian lane across from Covent Garden Opera.
ⓘ 25 🚇 Covent Garden

BLOOMSBURY
This area has a full range of good hotels, all within walking distance of the Bloomsbury museums, Covent Garden, and West End theaters.

■ St. Pancras Renaissance Hotel
£££££
EUSTON ROAD NW1
TEL 020 7841 3540
FAX 020 7841 3579
www.marriott.co.uk
The Midland Grand Hotel in St. Pancras Station was London's premier station-hotel before it closed in 1935. In its refurbished form, it is London's newest upscale hotel.
ⓘ 245 🚇 King's Cross St. Pancras

■ Charlotte Street Hotel
££££
15–17 CHARLOTTE STREET WC1
TEL 020 7806 2000
FAX 020 7806 2002
www.firmdale.com
A smart yet friendly and relaxed hotel inside a period

TRAVEL ESSENTIALS

building, with a small gym and the reliable Oscar restaurant.

① 52 **⊞** *Tottenham Court Road*

■ **The Montague on the Gardens**
££££
15 MONTAGUE STREET WC1
TEL 020 7637 1001
www.montaguehotel.com
Centrally located, this stylish hotel is imaginatively decorated, with attention to detail. Rooms offer bold decor and quality furnishings.

① 100 **⊞** *Holborn*

■ **Sanderson**
££££
50 BERNERS STREET W1
TEL 020 7300 1400
www.sandersonlondon.com
As with its sister hotel, St. Martin's Lane (see p. 183), the Schrager-Starck partnership creates minimalist rooms but crowded public spaces; try the Long Bar and the spa.

① 150 **⊞** *Oxford Circus*

■ **Academy**
£££
21 GOWER STREET WC1
TEL 020 7631 4115
www.theetoncollection.com
Set in five Georgian row houses, with opulent furnishings and discreet art, this fairy-tale view of English interiors works well.

① 49 **⊞** *Goodge Street*

■ **The Harlingford**
££
61–63 CARTWRIGHT GARDENS WC1
TEL 020 7387 1551
www.harlingfordhotel.com

Despite the budget rates, all guests enjoy en-suite bathrooms decorated in a contemporary style. The management is friendly, and there is an adjacent garden and even a tennis court.

① 44 **⊞** *Russell Square/Euston*

■ **Morgan Hotel**
££
24 BLOOMSBURY WC1
TEL 020 7636 3735
FAX 020 7636 3045
www.morganhotel.co.uk
Superbly located, this modest and good-value family-run hotel near the British Museum has both rooms and small apartments.

① 21 **⊞** *Tottenham Court Road*

■ **Generator**
£
37 TAVISTOCK PLACE WC1
TEL 020 7388 7666
FAX 020 7388 7644
www.generatorhostels.com
Steel, chrome, and exposed pipes—plus its huge size, lively bar, and Internet room—keep the setting sleek, the prices low, and the guests hip and happy. Mostly dorm-style rooms.

① 848 beds **⊞** *Russell Square*

KENSINGTON & SOUTH KENSINGTON

There are several town-house hotels in this residential area close to Hyde Park and some excellent museums.

■ **Baglioni**
£££££
60 HYDE PARK GATE SW7
TEL 020 7368 5700
www.baglionihotels.com

Inside a Victorian mansion opposite Kensington Palace, its atmosphere is easy, the decor chic modern, the rooms equipped with everything including espresso machines. There is a serious spa.

① 68 **⊞** *High Street Kensington*

■ **Aster House**
£££
3 SUMNER PLACE SW7
TEL 020 7581 5888
www.asterhouse.com
This welcoming hotel has excellent service, fine attention to detail, a garden with a duck pond, and a delightful, plant-filled conservatory setting for breakfast.

① 13 **⊞** *South Kensington*

■ **The Gore**
£££
190 QUEEN'S GATE SW7
TEL 020 7584 6601
www.gorehotel.com
Opened more than a century ago, the Gore carefully preserves its Victorian details with paneled rooms, potted ferns, rugs, and glorious stained-glass windows. The same building houses the fine-quality Bar One Ninety and Bistro One Ninety (*020 759 6705*).

① 50 **⊞** *South Kensington*

■ **The Sumner**
£££
54 UPPER BERKELEY STREET MARBLE ARCH W1
TEL 020 7723 2244
FAX 0870 7058767
www.thesumner.com
The excellent 5 Sumner Place hotel in South Kensington has morphed itself into a grander

refurbished town house in Marylebone, installing its notably caring staff.

ⓘ 20 🚇 Marble Arch

■ Gallery Hotel
££

8–10 QUEENSBERRY PLACE SW7
TEL 020 7915 0000
FAX 020 7915 4400
www.eeh.co.uk

This flagship hotel of the Elegant English Hotels chain (which includes the Gainsborough and Willett in London) offers good value service in well-furnished Victorian-era buildings.

ⓘ 36 🚇 South Kensington

■ London Vicarage Hotel
££

10 VICARAGE GATE W8
TEL 020 7229 4030
FAX 020 7792 5989
www.londonvicaragehotel.com

The grand lobby of this Victorian stucco town house leads to more restrained rooms, and the ambience is relaxed.

ⓘ 17 🚇 High Street Kensington/Notting Hill Gate

■ The Mayflower Hotel
££

26–28 TREBOVIR ROAD SW5
TEL 020 7370 0991
FAX 020 7370 0994
www.mayflowerhotel.co.uk

This hotel includes modern, well-appointed rooms, with a touch of the exotic, such as colonial ceiling fans. It also has adjoining apartments. Nearby are two sister hotels: Twenty Nevern Square Hotel and New Linden Hotel.

ⓘ 48 🚇 Earl's Court

■ The Rushmore Hotel
££

11 TREBOVIR ROAD SW5
TEL 020 7370 3839
FAX 020 7370 0274
www.rushmore-hotel.co.uk

Frescoed walls, draped beds, an elegant breakfast room, and good service make this hotel a bargain deal.

ⓘ 22 🚇 Earl's Court

CHELSEA, BELGRAVIA, & KNIGHTSBRIDGE

Stylish Londoners and foreign diplomats set the tone in one of London's plushest neighborhoods, with some discreet hotels.

■ The Berkeley
£££££

WILTON PLACE SW1
TEL 020 7235 6000
www.the-berkeley.co.uk

The Berkeley is a modern hotel run on traditional lines: open fire in the lobby, lavish flower arrangements, spacious rooms, valet service. Excellent top-floor health club and swimming pool, are equaled by the bar and restaurants that include Marcus Wareing's Pétrus.

ⓘ 214 🚇 Hyde Park Corner

■ The Capital
£££££

22 BASIL STREET
KNIGHTSBRIDGE SW3
TEL 020 7589 5171
FAX 020 7225 0011
www.capitalhotel.co.uk

Egyptian cotton sheets cover the beds in this immaculate, design-conscious hotel that has both rooms and apartments.

Eric Chavot cooks notably in the Capital restaurant.

ⓘ 49 🚇 Knightsbridge

■ The Goring
£££££

BEESTON PLACE
GROSVENOR GARDENS SW1
TEL 020 7396 9000
FAX 020 7834 4393
www.thegoring.com

Run by the Goring family since 1910, this hotel promises top-notch hospitality and service, and each room is individually designed and decorated. The excellent restaurant serves both traditional and contemporary British cuisine. The clublike bar is also first-rate.

ⓘ 71 🚇 Victoria

■ The Halkin
£££££

HALKIN STREET SW1
TEL 020 7333 1000
FAX 020 7333 1100
www.halkin.como.bz

This fashion-conscious hotel's decoration is inspired by classic Italian style—notably the good air-conditioning and lighting control and staff dressed in Armani. There is also a Michelin-starred contemporary Thai restaurant called Nahm.

ⓘ 41 🚇 Hyde Park Corner

■ Jumeirah Carlton Tower
£££££

CADOGAN PLACE SW1
TEL 020 7235 1234
FAX 020 7235 9129
www.jumeirah.com

An impressive modern hotel, whose sky-high swimming pool and health club indicate top-quality services at all levels; Chinoiserie Lounge for tea, Rib Room and Oyster Bar for traditional food. It is conveniently situated for Harrods and other shopping.

ⓘ 220 🚇 Knightsbridge

■ **The Lanesborough**
££££
HYDE PARK CORNER SW1
TEL 020 7259 5599
FAX 020 7259 5606
www.lanesborough.com
Located on Hyde Park Corner, this modern traditional hotel created inside a grand 19th-century neoclassical building offers lavish furnishings and extremely comfortable rooms. The Conservatory restaurant, with its palms and fountains, serves international cuisine. If you want to go all out, a butler service is available.

ⓘ 95 🚇 Hyde Park Corner

■ **Mandarin Oriental Hyde Park**
£££££
66 KNIGHTSBRIDGE SW1
TEL 020 7235 2000
FAX 020 7235 2001
www.mandarinoriental.com
A splendid Edwardian landmark, extravagantly refurbished. The large rooms (request a view of Hyde Park), have lavish bathrooms. Two outstanding restaurants include the French Bar Boulud, overseen by Daniel Boulud, and the first London venture from Britain's own three-Michelin-star chef, Heston Blumenthal, called Dinner by Heston Blumenthal.

ⓘ 198 🚇 Knightsbridge

■ **The Knightsbridge**
££££
10 BEAUFORT GARDENS SW3
TEL 020 7584 6300
FAX 020 7584 6355
www.firmdale.com
Situated in a good location for Knightsbridge shopping, with upscale rooms to match. No bar, restaurant, or gym, but a great room-service menu.

ⓘ 44 🚇 Knightsbridge

■ **The Rockwell**
£££
181–183 CROMWELL ROAD, SW5
TEL 020 7244 2000
www.therockwell.com
One of London's best recent openings occupies a listed historic building. Rooms are all different, though all share elegant and understated contemporary styling.

ⓘ 40 🚇 Earl's Court

■ **B&B Belgravia**
££
64–66 EBURY STREET SW1
TEL 020 7259 8570
FAX 020 7259 8591
www.bb-belgravia.com
Away from chintz, this is freshness and contemporary quality introducing a new understanding of a "B&B," from quality bed linen and power showers to fresh breakfast ingredients.

ⓘ 17 🚇 Victoria

■ **Morgan Guest House**
££
120 EBURY STREET SW1
TEL 020 7730 2384
www.morganhouse.co.uk
A charming bed-and-breakfast home in pretty, well-located Pimlico; good

breakfasts; some rooms share bathrooms. Includes rooms for up to four people.

ⓘ 11 🚇 Victoria

EAST LONDON

The revitalization of East London has transformed it into one of the coolest parts of the city, with a lively arts scene and street markets.

■ **Four Seasons Canary Wharf**
£££££
46 WESTFERRY CIRCUS E14
TEL 020 7510 1999
FAX 020 7510 1998
www.fourseasons.com
Canary Wharf's first deluxe hotel pampers guests with all modern conveniences including pool, spa, and tennis courts.

ⓘ 142 🚇 Canary Wharf

■ **The Zetter Hotel**
££££
86–88 CLERKENWELL ROAD EC1
TEL 020 7324 4444
www.thezetter.com
This cool loft-hotel, in a restored 19th-century warehouse, is decorated with 1970s furniture, old books, and modern technology.

ⓘ 59 🚇 Farringdon

■ **The Hoxton**
£££
81 GREAT EASTERN STREET EC2
TEL 020 7550 1090
www.hoxtonhotels.com
One of London's trendiest neighborhoods has one of its trendiest hotels, decorated with work from local artists.

ⓘ 205 🚇 Shoreditch High Street

INDEX

INDEX

INDEX

CREDITS

Walking London

Published by the National Geographic Society
John M. Fahey, Jr., *Chairman of the Board and Chief Executive Officer*
Timothy T. Kelly, *President*
Declan Moore, *Executive Vice President; President, Publishing*
Melina Gerosa Bellows, *Executive Vice President, Chief Creative Officer, Books, Kids, and Family*

Prepared by the Book Division
Barbara Brownell Grogan, *Vice President and Editor in Chief*
Jonathan Halling, *Design Director, Books and Children's Publishing*
Marianne R. Koszorus, *Design Director, Books*
Barbara A. Noe, *Senior Editor*
Carl Mehler, *Director of Maps*
Lawrence M. Porges, *Project Editor*
Marty Ittner, *Design Consultant*
Leslie Allen, Lise Sajewski, Anne Smyth, *Contributors*
R. Gary Colbert, *Production Director*
Mike Horenstein, *Production Manager*
Jennifer A. Thornton, *Managing Editor*
Meredith C. Wilcox, *Administrative Director, Illustrations*

Travel Publications
Keith Bellows, *Vice President and Editor in Chief*
Jerry Sealy, *Director of Design*

Manufacturing and Quality Management
Christopher A. Liedel, *Chief Financial Officer*
Phillip L. Schlosser, *Senior Vice President*
Chris Brown, *Technical Director*
Nicole Elliott, *Manager*
Rachel Faulise, *Manager*
Robert L. Barr, *Manager*

Created by Toucan Books Ltd
Ellen Dupont, *Editorial Director*
Helen Douglas-Cooper, *Senior Editor*
Peter Clubb, Jane Hutchings, Andrew Kerr-Jarrett, Alice Peebles, *Editors*
Leah Germann, *Designer*
Christine Vincent, *Picture Manager*
Sharon Southren, *Picture Researcher*
Merritt Cartographic, *Maps*
Beth Landis Hester, *Proofreader*
Marie Lorimer, *Indexer*

The National Geographic Society is one of the world's largest nonprofit scientific and educational organizations. Founded in 1888 to "increase and diffuse geographic knowledge," the Society works to inspire people to care about the planet. National Geographic reflects the world through its magazines, television programs, films, music and radio, books, DVDs, maps, exhibitions, live events, school publishing programs, interactive media and merchandise. *National Geographic* magazine, the Society's official journal, published in English and 33 local-language editions, is read by more than 40 million people each month. The National Geographic Channel reaches 370 million households in 34 languages in 168 countries. National Geographic Digital Media receives more than 15 million visitors a month. National Geographic has funded more than 9,600 scientific research, conservation and exploration projects and supports an education program promoting geography literacy. For more information, visit www.nationalgeographic.com.

For more information, please call 1-800-NGS LINE (647-5463) or write to the following address:

National Geographic Society
1145 17th Street N.W.
Washington, D.C. 20036-4688 U.S.A.

For information about special discounts for bulk purchases, please contact National Geographic Books Special Sales: ngspecsales@ngs.org

For rights or permissions inquiries, please contact National Geographic Books Subsidiary Rights: ngbookrights@ngs.org

ISBN: 978-1-4262-0870-6

Printed in Italy

11/MV/1

The information in this book has been carefully checked and is, to the best of our knowledge, accurate as of press time. It's always advisable to call ahead, however, as details are subject to change. The National Geographic Society cannot be responsible for any changes, or for errors or omissions.